QUIVERTREE
PUBLICATIONS

lazy days

contemporary country-style cooking

by phillippa cheifitz

photography by craig fraser

contents

CHAPTER ONE
on the road

For me the holiday mood begins at the sign to Groote Post, one of the best of the West Coast wine farms. Every now and again we take the winding road to stock up at the cellar.

There's a choice of farm stalls on the way where we pick up country breads — well-risen puffed whites and wholesome brown loaves. Then there are homemade jams, farm butter, newly laid eggs, biltong, lemon syrup and ginger beer. And at my favourite Weskus Spens Padstal, homemade feta. We make one last stop at the charming Die Winkel op Paternoster for homemade rusks to dip in early-morning coffee, biscuits for tea, korrelkonfyt for the smoked snoek, pickles, poached quince slices and sun-dried homegrown pears.

Once we get to the beach house, I can't wait to cut a thick slice of bread. If it's mid-morning it needs a good smear of farm butter and homemade apricot jam along with a pot of bush tea. Nearer to lunch, something savoury; shredded biltong or cheese and pickles, perhaps smoked snoek and a dab of korrelkonfyt. A tall glass of lemon syrup, gin, sparkling mineral water, lots of ice and mint. Or ginger beer with gin and a drizzle of grenadine on the rocks.

anchovy butter

100g unsalted butter
squeeze of lemon juice
50g can or 1 small bottle anchovies, drained
milled black pepper

Blend or process all ingredients together. To serve, spread on fresh bread or hot toast.
For 6

tuna spread

200g can tuna in oil
50g butter, at room temperature
lemon juice
sea salt
milled black pepper

Blend or process the tuna and its oil with the butter. Add a good squeeze of lemon juice and season the spread to taste.
For 6

rocket, sun-dried pear and feta salad with hot pecans and red wine vinegar dressing

Allow one generous handful of rocket per serving. Toss with a little olive oil, sea salt and milled pepper. Add a drizzle of red wine vinegar. Turn onto large plates, or a single platter. Add thinly sliced sun-dried pear, about one pear per person, and feta, broken into large pieces. Drizzle the feta pieces with a little olive oil and add a twist of pepper. Oven-toast some pecans at 180°C for about 10 minutes, or dry-fry in a hot pan, and add a few to each plate.

In summer, when the sun sets late, we leave town after work. Then I need something quick for dinner, so I pick up good beef steaks – or fresh fish – on the way.

simplest steaks

2 beef steaks, rib-eye or aged rump, about 200g each
sea salt and milled black pepper
olive oil

For serving:
watercress, mustard, roasted potato wedges or buttery mash

Oil the steaks and season with salt. Heat a ridged cast-iron pan. When hot, sear the steaks on both sides until nice and brown. (If there's an edge of fat, brown the fat side first.) Once seared, place in the oven, heated to 180°C, for 5 minutes. Turn off the heat and leave to rest in the oven for another 5 minutes. Season with black pepper, garnish with watercress drizzled with a little olive oil and serve with mustard and potatoes.
For 2

seared rib-eye steaks with avocado sauce

2 rib-eye steaks, about 200g each
sea salt and milled black pepper
olive oil

For the sauce, roughly mash together:
1 large ripe avocado pear
good squeeze lemon juice
1 fresh green chilli, chopped
1 clove garlic, crushed
handful of coriander leaves, chopped
sea salt and milled black pepper

For serving:
baked sweet potatoes

Moisten the steaks with oil and season. Sear over a fairly high heat until well browned on both sides but rare inside. Wrap in foil and rest for 5 minutes. Serve with the sauce and baked sweet potatoes.
For 2

grilled fish steaks with herbs

2 thick fish steaks, about 180g each
sea salt and milled black pepper
olive oil
sprigs of thyme, oregano and rosemary

For serving:
lime or lemon wedges, slim crisp fries

Pat the fish steaks dry, season lightly and moisten generously with olive oil. Place on a bed of fresh herbs in a suitably sized grill pan that has been lightly oiled. Slide under a hot grill for 5–7 minutes, without turning, or until browned and just cooked through. Lift onto 2 hot plates. Drizzle with olive oil. At the table, squeeze over lime or lemon juice and add a little sea salt and a twist of black pepper. Serve with slim crisp fries.
For 2

glazed lamb steaks with beetroot salsa

4 lamb steaks, about 500g, or 8 lamb rib chops
sea salt and milled black pepper
olive oil
rocket leaves

For the glaze:
3 tablespoons dry red wine
1/2 cup balsamic vinegar
1 tablespoon soft brown sugar

Simmer together for about 5 minutes until reduced and syrupy.

For the beetroot salsa, mix together:
250g cooked beetroot, peeled and chopped
1–2 tablespoons chopped red onion
1 tablespoon red wine vinegar
2 tablespoons lemon juice
1–2 tablespoons chopped coriander
1 fresh green chilli, chopped (optional)
sea salt and milled black pepper

For garnishing:
rocket leaves

Trim excess fat from the lamb, then season and moisten with oil. Heat a ridged cast-iron pan over a high heat. First brown the fat side, then sear the lamb for a minute or two on each side until charred but still very rare. Remove and coat with the glaze. Bake at 180°C for 5 minutes. Turn off the heat and leave to rest for 5 minutes. Garnish generously with rocket leaves and serve with the beetroot salsa.
For 2–4

mayonnaise

I use the fresh farm eggs I've purchased to make a quick blender mayonnaise. I use whole eggs and a hand-held electric stick blender to make a light and fluffy mayonnaise.

STEP 1. In the blender cup or a bowl, place 1 whole free-range egg, a pinch of salt, a grinding of pepper and 1 tablespoon of lemon juice or wine vinegar. If you like, add 1 teaspoon of Dijon mustard or a pinch of English mustard powder.

STEP 2. Slowly whizz in sunflower or canola oil.

STEP 3. Keep going until the mayonnaise is thick and smooth. If it seems too thick, blend in a tablespoon of boiling water. This mayonnaise will keep, sealed and in the refrigerator, for up to a week. **Makes about 1 cup**

variations

- Use 2 egg yolks instead of the whole egg if you want a richer, denser consistency that is suitable for spreading on oven-toasts to float on a fish soup.
- Sunflower or canola oil is chosen for its lightness, but you can add a few tablespoons of olive oil towards the end of blending, especially for Mediterranean-style dishes.
- If flavouring with garlic, stir freshly crushed garlic into the finished mayonnaise.
- For a spicy mayonnaise, blend in 1 teaspoon chilli paste. Stir in a few drops of Tabasco at the end if you think it needs even more bite.

beans

I love the local dried beans that I pick up at the farm stall. As soon as I've unpacked, I cover the beans in water to soak overnight. To cook, drain first, then cover with lots of fresh water and bring to the boil in a suitable saucepan. For 500g beans, add 1 chopped onion, 2 smashed cloves garlic, 1 or 2 sprigs rosemary, 3 or 4 sprigs thyme and a bay leaf. Don't add salt, which toughens the beans. Bring to the boil and allow to boil for 5–10 minutes, then reduce the heat and simmer, adding more boiling water if necessary. When the beans start to soften, stir in 1 tablespoon olive oil. Cook until soft, then stir in 1 tablespoon salt and cook for another 10 minutes or so. Stir now and again to prevent the beans from sticking.

bean salad with onion, tomato and red wine vinegar dressing

While the beans are still warm, toss with a dressing of 2 tablespoons red wine vinegar, 1/3–1/2 cup olive oil, 1–2 crushed cloves garlic, sea salt and milled black pepper to taste. Sprinkle with a confetti of finely chopped sweet onion, tomato and parsley or shredded basil leaves. I sometimes add a fistful of olives and some crumbled feta.
For 8

bean soup with anchovy cream and garlic croutons

3 tablespoons olive oil
1 onion, finely chopped
1 carrot, finely chopped
1/4 cup chopped celery
1 bay leaf
a few sprigs parsley
a few sprigs thyme
sea salt and milled black pepper
1 fat clove garlic, crushed
500g dried beans, cooked and drained
12 cups vegetable or chicken stock

In a suitable saucepan, heat the oil. Gently cook onion, carrot, celery and herbs with a little salt until softened. Stir in the garlic, then the beans and allow to cook gently for a few minutes. Pour in the stock and bring to a bubble. Reduce the heat and simmer for about 2 hours. If necessary, add more stock from time to time, and stir now and again to prevent catching. Check seasoning. Thin down with extra stock if too thick. After standing, you may also need to add more liquid. If you like, use a stick blender to give the soup a good consistency; not too smooth though, as it should have some texture.

For the anchovy cream:
1/2 cup cream
1 clove garlic
4 anchovy fillets, chopped

Simmer the ingredients together for a few minutes until the anchovies have disintegrated.

For serving:
homemade croutons, chopped Italian parsley

Drizzle anchovy cream over each serving of soup and add a sprinkling of parsley. Serve the homemade croutons on the side.
For 8

Note: to make homemade croutons, lightly toast thick slices of day-old bread and trim the crusts. Cut into small cubes and fry in shallow hot oil in a non-stick pan, not too many at a time and stirring often until golden. Add more oil as needed. If you like, add a knob of butter too. Drain on paper towels. Alternatively, toast the cubes in the oven at 180°C for about 15 minutes. Either toss them in oil before baking or simply leave them dry.

bean mash

A soft mound of mash made of beans, lentils or chickpeas makes a perfect bed for a grilled chop or saucy stew.

Roughly blend 500g hot cooked beans with a hand-held electric stick blender, gradually adding 1/4–1/2 cup olive oil. Stir in 2 crushed cloves garlic and seasoning to taste. If it seems too thick, thin down with a little boiling water or stock, or more oil.
For 8 as a side dish

baked beans

In an ovenproof casserole, gently cook 2 thinly sliced onions in a mix of butter and olive oil until softened. Stir in 2 crushed cloves garlic, 2 tablespoons tomato paste, a bay leaf, a sprig or two of rosemary and some thyme, and seasoning. Add the cooked beans and mix well together. Pour over a cup of dry red wine or stock, cover with a sheet of oiled greaseproof paper and bake at 160°C for 30 minutes. Serve with a green salad, topped with a mushroom ragout, or place a just-roasted leg of lamb on top of the beans before baking.
For 8

pea soup with ham

1 kg smoked ham hock
500g dried split peas
10 cups water
1 teaspoon mustard powder
1 teaspoon dried oregano
2 onions, chopped
4–6 carrots, chopped
3–4 sticks celery, chopped
3–4 tablespoons chopped parsley
salt and milled black pepper

Bring the ham and water to a bubble in a large casserole, then skim the surface. Add the rest of the ingredients and simmer for 2 hours or until the meat is very tender and the peas are reduced to a puree, adding more water if necessary. Season to taste. Chill to solidify the fat, then remove. Pull the meat off the bone into large shreds, discarding skin, fat and bone. Return to the soup and gently reheat. If necessary, thin down with water or stock. Check seasoning and serve.
For 8

Wines purchased on the way to Paternoster are soon uncorked to use for gutsy marinades, gentler casseroles, or to add depth to syrups.

chicken and vegetable casserole with white wine, thyme and black olives

8 chicken portions, about 1kg
2 tablespoons olive oil
sea salt and milled black pepper
400g baby onions, skinned and halved
400g baby potatoes, halved
2 cloves garlic, crushed
2 tablespoons tomato paste
1 cup dry white wine
2 cups chicken stock
200g baby carrots, trimmed
200g baby green beans, trimmed
a handful of fresh thyme
a handful of ripe black olives

Trim the chicken portions, rinse and dry well. In a large heavy casserole, sauté chicken in heated oil until nicely browned, then remove and set aside. Season lightly. Stir onions and potatoes around in the fat left in the pan. Stir in the garlic and tomato paste. Pour in wine and stock and bring to a bubble. Return chicken portions to the pan along with the rest of the vegetables. Add a little seasoning, then the thyme and olives. Reduce the heat and simmer, covered, for 45 minutes or until chicken and vegetables are tender. If necessary, add more stock during cooking. Check seasoning and serve.
For 4

wine-poached pears

You could choose honey to sweeten the pears rather than sugar. If you like your pears spiced, add the suggested list of flavourings – and poach in red wine if including the spices. These pears are perfect served with runny Brie and biscuits.

8 medium brown pears
1 1/2 cups sugar (brown or white)
3 cups dry red or white wine
1 1/2 cups water

Optional flavourings:
4 cloves
2 or 3 star anise
3 sticks cinnamon
1 teaspoon coriander seeds
grating of nutmeg
1 orange, sliced
2 bay leaves
1 lemon, sliced

Peel the pears, leaving the stalks on. Stir the sugar, wine and water together in a medium saucepan (bear in mind that the pears need to be covered in liquid when poaching) and bring to the boil. Add the optional flavourings, if using, and then the pears. Place a round of greaseproof paper directly on the surface. (A lid or plate on top of this will keep the pears submerged.) Simmer for 15 minutes or until tender when pierced with the tip of a knife. Turn off the heat and leave to cool, covered, in the liquid. Remove the pears with a slotted spoon and reduce the poaching liquid over a high heat for 5–10 minutes or until syrupy. If you want to cut the sweetness, add the strained juice of a lemon or two – or in autumn, a squeeze of fresh pomegranate juice. Pour the reduced glaze over the pears and allow to cool, then chill well. Serve with cheese and biscuits.
For 8

simple jam tart

With my newly acquired jars of homemade jam, I love to make a simple tart for afternoon tea. I use an easy pastry, rich with thick sour cream and farm butter.

For the pastry:
200g butter
200ml thick sour cream
2 cups flour

For the filling:
1 cup homemade jam
1 tablespoon lemon juice

For serving:
cream, fresh or sour

Cream the butter and sour cream together, then mix in the flour to make a soft dough. Wrap well and chill for an hour or until firm enough to roll. Roll out thinly between 2 sheets of lightly floured baking paper. Allow to rest in the fridge while heating the oven to 190°C. Roll out evenly and cut out a 30cm round. Remove the scraps and lift the round with the paper onto a baking sheet. Re-roll the scraps. Chill again to firm, then cut out 8 strips. Mix the jam with the lemon juice and spread over the circle of pastry, leaving a border. Fold in the edges of the pastry to form a rim. Cover the jam filling with strips of pastry, criss-crossed and interleaved, trimming the ends to fit. Bake at 190°C for about half an hour or until golden brown. Allow to cool to room temperature, but serve freshly baked, with cream.
For 8

baked cinnamon-chocolate custards

2 cups full cream milk
100g dark chocolate, broken into bits
1 free-range egg
3 free-range egg yolks
1/3 cup icing sugar
1 teaspoon vanilla extract
1 teaspoon ground cinnamon
icing sugar and cocoa for dusting

Gently heat the milk with the chocolate until the latter has melted. Whisk the egg and yolks, then beat in the chocolate-milk mix, sugar, vanilla and cinnamon. Strain and pour into 6 ovenproof ramekins. Place in a baking pan with enough hot water to come halfway up the sides. Bake at 150°C for 45 minutes or until set. Dust with a mix of icing sugar and cocoa. Serve warm, at room temperature or chilled.
For 6

CHAPTER TWO
at home

I suppose you'd call this family food, the kind
of food we cook for ourselves or for family on Saturdays.
In summer we go for an early walk, when it's still cool, then
breakfast (or call it brunch) late. Winter walks generally follow
breakfast. Either way, good coffee and a rusk for dunking starts
the day. A good tea in the afternoon and a comforting
dish for supper is the general pattern.

bacon and egg pies

For each pie:
1 x 10cm square puff pastry
1 free-range egg
2 rashers bacon

Cut strips off the edges of each square of pastry. Brush each square with water, then press on the strips, trimming to fit, to make a raised border. Bake at 200°C for 5 minutes. Bake the bacon separately at the same time. Remove and cool slightly. Drop an egg onto each pastry square and add the bacon. Bake for 15 minutes or until the egg is just set and the pastry is puffed and golden.

french toast

4 free-range eggs
1 cup full-cream milk
4 slices white country bread
a mix of butter and sunflower oil for frying

Beat the eggs and milk together. Turn into a wide shallow bowl. Prick the sliced bread all over with a fork. Dip into the egg-and-milk mixture. Turn until the bread is nice and soggy. Shallow-fry, over a medium heat, in a mix of hot butter and oil, until golden brown on both sides. Serve as is or with a drizzle of honey.
For 4

Note: to make French toast sandwiches for brunch or lunch, sandwich the soaked bread with sliced baked ham and Gruyère, a smear of mustard and a grinding of black pepper. Or use sliced tomato and mozzarella, lightly seasoned. Fry the whole sandwich in a mix of butter and oil over a medium heat, pressing down with a spatula, until the sandwich is golden brown on both sides and the egg is cooked through.

basic onion confit

3 tablespoons unsalted butter
2 tablespoons olive oil
1 kg peeled onions, thinly sliced
grating of nutmeg (optional)
sea salt and milled black pepper

Melt the butter and olive oil, add the onions and cook, covered, for 40 minutes or until reduced, meltingly tender and still pale. If you like, add some nutmeg. Season to taste.

The basic onion confit can be used in a number of ways. You could, for example, simply bake the confit in a buttered dish for 15 minutes at 200°C, then turn on the grill to brown the top. Serve with sliced ham, a green salad and crusty bread. It's delicious spread on the bread. You can also enrich the confit by mixing it with 2 eggs and 1/3 cup cream before baking to make a kind of crustless quiche.
For 6–8

baked eggs with onion confit

Spoon onion confit into shallow, ovenproof baking dishes just the right size to take an egg. Sprinkle some chopped ham or anchovies onto the confit, break an egg on top, then cover with a film of cream and some grated Gruyère. Bake at 190°C for 10–15 minutes or until the egg is just set. Serve immediately.

onion-confit tarts

To make the tart pastry, lightly knead together:
1 1/4 cups flour
1 1/4 cups grated Gruyère
150g butter

Pat the dough into six 12cm tart tins. Prick and freeze while heating the oven to 200°C. Bake for 8 minutes or until pale golden. Cool before adding the filling.

For the onion confit filling:
basic onion confit
2 free-range eggs, beaten
1/3 cup thick cream
sea salt and milled black pepper
grating of nutmeg (optional)

Mix the onion confit with the beaten eggs and cream. Season to taste. Bake for 25 minutes or until set. If using, grate nutmeg over the top of each tart.
Makes 6

winter vegetable and barley soup with deep-fried toast soldiers

4 slices neck of lamb (about 600g)
sunflower oil
1 onion, chopped
1 bunch leeks, sliced
2 sticks celery, sliced
sea salt and milled black pepper
1 clove garlic, chopped
3–4 turnips, peeled and cut into chunks
4–5 carrots, peeled and cut into chunks
4–6 parsnips, peeled and cut into chunks
1 cup barley, rinsed
12 cups vegetable stock or water
handful of chopped parsley

For serving:
chopped parsley, deep-fried toast soldiers

Remove any excess fat from the lamb. In a large saucepan, brown the pieces of lamb in a minimum of oil. Remove and pour off the fat. Add a tablespoon or two of fresh oil, and over a gentle heat simmer the onion, leeks and celery with a pinch of salt until softened. Stir in the garlic. Return the lamb to the pot, then add the vegetables, barley and stock. Add a spoonful of salt and a grinding of black pepper. Bring to a bubble, then reduce the heat. Skim off any scum. Add the parsley. Simmer gently, almost covered, for about 2 hours or until the meat is falling off the bone. If necessary, add more stock or water from time to time during cooking. Check seasoning. If it thickens too much on standing, loosen with extra stock.

To make the toast soldiers, deep-fry strips of lightly toasted day–old bread in hot oil until golden and crisp. Drain on paper towels and serve while still warm, with the soup.
For 6–8

herbed pasta squares

1 cup imported Italian 00 flour (available at speciality food shops)
1/2 teaspoon salt
1 large free-range egg, lightly beaten
2 tablespoons warm water
Italian parsley or basil

STEP 1. Sift the flour and salt onto a large slab of marble or a board, or use a large bowl. Make a decent dent in the middle and pour in the lightly beaten egg and water.

STEP 2. Stir together, then knead to make a stiff but smooth dough. Knead for about 5 minutes to ensure its elasticity. If necessary, dampen your hands with warm water to add a little extra moisture as you knead. Wrap in plastic and leave to rest for an hour.

STEP 3. To roll the dough, divide it into 2 pieces, roughly flattening each one. Dust the piece you're using with flour, but keep the rest covered. You could patiently roll it out by hand, but your best bet is a hand-operated pasta machine. Start with the plain rollers of the machine opened to the widest setting. Tuck in any untidy edges and fold in half or thirds. Dust with flour and put through the machine again, and again if necessary, until you have a smooth sheet.

STEP 4. Turning the machine down a notch at a time, roll the dough until it reaches the thinness you require. When the sheet of pasta becomes too long to handle, cut it in half.

STEP 5. Sandwich the parsley or basil between two pasta sheets. Roll through the machine once more and cut into squares.

STEP 6. The simplest way to serve these squares is to cook them in gently simmering vegetable or chicken broth (it's worth making your own; see page 49) until they are just tender. Ladle into bowls and dust with freshly and finely grated Italian Parmesan cheese.

Note: this quantity of pasta also makes enough for one generous portion of plain cut pasta, from broad tagliatelle to fine angel hair.

chicken broth

Delicious on its own, with the herbed pasta squares floating in it or used as a base for other soups, this is not as smart as a professional stock – rather, it's a simple broth that adds an extra dimension to home cooking.

1 whole free-range chicken or 800g–1kg chicken wings
1 large onion
about 10 cups cold water
6–8 whole carrots, peeled
1 celery heart, halved
handful of celery leaves, roughly chopped
1 bay leaf
handful of parsley
1 tablespoon salt
a few black peppercorns

Optional extras:
1 or 2 whole ripe red tomatoes
a chunk of pumpkin
some garlic cloves, unpeeled and smashed

If using a whole chicken, cut out the breasts and freeze to use another time. Cut the rest of the chicken in half and place in a large pot with the onion and cold water. Gently bring to the boil, then skim the surface. Stir in the remaining ingredients and cook very gently, half-covered, for about 2 hours. Strain and check seasoning. If serving as a soup, reduce a little if necessary to intensify the flavour, or add a good quality chicken stock cube. Alastair Little, an English chef I admire, adds a few stock cubes at the beginning.

Note: anyone with fastidious taste would discard the boiled chicken, but I enjoy eating it with the carrots and celery heart while it's all still warm, with a little coarse sea salt, milled pepper and mustard. The chicken wings, sprinkled with soy sauce, sesame oil and chopped spring onion, also make a tasty cook's treat.
Makes 6–8 cups

homemade italian-style tomato sauce

1 large onion
2–3 tablespoons olive oil
3–4 cloves garlic, crushed
1,5 kg ripe red tomatoes, skinned, seeded and chopped
sea salt and milled black pepper
2–3 tablespoons shredded basil leaves or chopped Italian parsley

Gently cook the onion in the oil until softened but pale in colour. Stir in the garlic, then the tomatoes. Season, cover and simmer gently for about 1 1/2 hours. Serve as is, or blend to form a smooth thick sauce. Or if you prefer, uncover and reduce over a high heat to create a thick chunky consistency. Stir in the herbs and check seasoning. The sauce freezes well, so you could prepare a big batch and divide into single-portion containers.
For 6

cheese and tomato pancakes

about 8 thin pancakes, cooked on one side only

For the filling, mix together:
1 soft ball mozzarella, shredded
1/2 cup crumbled ricotta
1/4 cup grated Parmesan cheese
1/2 teaspoon dried oregano or some shredded basil leaves

For the topping:
about 1 cup homemade tomato sauce
a few tablespoons grated Parmesan cheese

Place some cheese filling on the cooked side of each pancake and roll up. Arrange in an oiled baking dish and spoon the tomato sauce over. Sprinkle with Parmesan cheese and bake for about 20 minutes at 190°C or until hot and golden.
For 4

roast chicken with herbs and potatoes

Serve with a mix of baby salad leaves or lots of watercress, tossed in a minimum of oil, a little wine vinegar, sea salt and milled pepper.

1 large free-range chicken, 1.5kg
sea salt and milled black pepper
1 lemon
a bunch of fresh mixed herbs – thyme, oregano, rosemary, sage and parsley
butter (optional)
olive oil
1 onion, thinly sliced
2 cloves garlic, crushed
4 large potatoes

For serving:
a mix of baby salad leaves or watercress

Split the chicken down the back and open out as flat as possible. Rinse and pat dry. Season with salt and pepper and squeeze the lemon juice over. Push some of the herbs under the skin of the breast of the chicken and some butter as well, or if you prefer, moisten with olive oil. Grease a roasting pan with olive oil. Place the chicken skin-side up on a bed of the rest of the herbs, the onion and the garlic. Drizzle the skin with a little olive oil. Scrub, or peel, and halve the potatoes. Place around the chicken. Roast, uncovered, at 200–220°C for an hour or until the skin is golden and crisp and the chicken tender.
For 4

deep-dish roast chicken and vegetable pies

The better the pastry, the better the pie. But life's not perfect, so if homemade is out, use a good quality store-bought one, all the easier when ready-rolled. Take care with the stock you use: a homemade broth is good, but the bones and vegetables will definitely improve a well-diluted cube.

4 chicken breasts, with skin and bone
sea salt and milled black pepper
olive oil
4 cups chicken stock
1/2 cup dry white wine
1 onion, thinly sliced
1 punnet whole baby carrots, peeled
1 punnet slim baby leeks, trimmed
6 short sticks celery, halved lengthwise
1 punnet baby parsnips, peeled and halved lengthwise
2 cloves garlic, chopped
handful of parsley
sprigs of thyme
a few peppercorns
1 bay leaf
1 1/2 tablespoons potato flour
juice of 2 lemons
beaten egg
1 sheet puff pastry

Rinse, pat dry, season and oil the chicken. Place in a large oiled roasting pan on top of a layer of onion, garlic and thyme. Roast at 230°C, one shelf above the middle, for 20–25 minutes or until golden but still moist and tender. Allow to cool. Tear the chicken into long pieces, removing bones, and set aside. Simmer the chicken bones with the stock, wine, vegetables, garlic, parsley, thyme, peppercorns and bay leaf for about 20 minutes or until the vegetables are just tender. Strain and season. Return 3 cups of broth to the heat. Whisk the potato flour with a little water to make a paste. Whisk into the hot broth and keep whisking until slightly thickened. Add lemon juice to taste. Place the chicken and vegetables in 4–6 individual pie dishes, oiled or buttered. Pour the lemony broth over the chicken and vegetables. Brush the edges of each pie dish with beaten egg and top the edges with strips of pastry. Brush these with egg, then cover with pastry 'lids', pressing the edges together well to seal. Brush pastry with beaten egg. Poke a hole in each pie so steam can escape. Bake at 220°C for about 25 minutes or until pastry is cooked through and golden.
For 4–6

cauliflower-cheese soufflés

1 medium cauliflower
2 cups vegetable stock
strained juice of 1 lemon
butter for greasing
3 tablespoons butter
3 tablespoons flour
1 cup warm full-cream milk
sea salt and milled black pepper
4 free-range eggs, separated
2 cups grated Gruyère
1 teaspoon Dijon mustard
grating of nutmeg
extra grated Gruyère for sprinkling
sprig or two of rosemary to garnish

Break the cauliflower into large florets. Soak in salted water for 5–10 minutes. Simmer in 2 cups vegetable stock with the lemon juice for 15 minutes or until just tender. Drain, but reserve 1/2 cup of the stock. Butter 3–4 ovenproof soup bowls. Divide the cauliflower between the prepared dishes. Melt 3 tablespoons butter. Stir in the flour until smooth. Remove from the heat, and gradually add the warm reserved stock and milk until blended. Season. Return to the heat and, stirring all the time, cook until thick and smooth. Remove from the heat and season. Lightly beat the egg yolks, then gradually whisk in. Stir in the grated Gruyère, mustard and nutmeg. Stiffly beat the egg whites and fold in. Divide the mixture between the soup bowls. Sprinkle with extra grated Gruyère. Bake at 200°C for 15 minutes or until puffed and golden. Reduce the heat to 180°C and bake for 5–10 minutes or until set. Serve immediately.
For 3–4

savoury mushroom bread-and-butter pudding

20g dried porcini mushrooms
1 cup warm vegetable broth
about 100g soft butter
8 thick slices farm-style white bread
4 whole free-range eggs
2 egg yolks
1 cup cream
2–3 tablespoons chopped dill, parsley and chives
250g fresh porcini or portabellini mushrooms
1 clove garlic, crushed
sea salt and milled black pepper

Soak the dried mushrooms in the broth for about 20 minutes. Butter the bread, trim the crusts and cut into triangles. Place in a buttered ovenproof dish. Beat eggs and yolks with the cream and the strained soaking broth. Add seasoning to taste, then the herbs. Chop the soaked mushrooms and the cleaned fresh ones and stir-fry in about 2 tablespoons butter until just cooked. Stir in the garlic. Season to taste. Allow to cool, then spread on the buttered bread. Arrange in a buttered baking dish and pour over the custard. Allow to soak for about an hour. Dot with butter. Place the dish in a baking tray of hot water and bake at 160°C for 1–1 1/4 hours until set, slightly puffed and golden. Serve as a starter, garnished with wild rocket, or as a main course with a green salad.
For 6

spinach and cheese pancakes

250g frozen chopped spinach, defrosted
2 tablespoons thick cream
125g Gruyère, grated
sea salt and milled black pepper
about 8 thin pancakes
butter
extra grated Gruyère or Parmesan cheese

Heat the spinach in a nonstick pan, stirring until all the moisture has evaporated. Stir in cream and cheese and check seasoning. Place a generous spoonful of filling in each pancake, then fold into quarters. Place on a well-buttered baking tray. Sprinkle all the pancakes with extra cheese and dot each one with butter. Bake at 200°C for 10–15 minutes or until hot and golden.
For 4

sweet wine jellies

Use the same recipe for those who don't drink alcohol – simply substitute grape juice for the wine.

3 leaves gelatine
2 cups sweet wine (white or red)

Soak the gelatine in cold water until softened. Heat a little of the wine, then stir in the squeezed-out gelatine leaves until dissolved. Stir in the rest of the wine. Strain. Pour into glasses and refrigerate until set. As a variation, try setting whole poached pears (see page 32) in the jelly. Peaches or fresh berries would be good too.
For 4

honeycomb mould

3 free-range eggs, separated
1 tablespoon gelatine
1/2 cup caster sugar
1/2 cup cream
grated rind and strained juice of 2 lemons
2 cups full-cream milk

Lightly beat the egg yolks. Add the gelatine and sugar and beat until thick and fluffy. Beat in the cream. Add the grated lemon rind to the milk and heat until bubbles form around the edge of the pan. Whisk the hot milk into the egg-yolk mixture. Cook over a gentle heat, stirring constantly, until the mixture is thick enough to coat the back of a spoon. Mix in the strained lemon juice and fold in the stiffly beaten egg whites. Pour into a wetted jelly mould and refrigerate until set.
For 6

country pancakes

I love an old-fashioned thickish pancake, straight out of the pan, spread with a good spoonful of homemade jam – apricot's my favourite – then rolled up, halved across if large and sprinkled with crunchy sugar and cinnamon. Squeeze a wedge of lemon over and eat... I make a jug of batter on Saturday and use it during the weekend. It's best to let the batter stand, even for half an hour. If the batter seems too thick when you come to use it, add iced water until it's the consistency of thin cream.

For the batter:
8 farm eggs or 6 extra-large free-range eggs
1/4 teaspoon salt
1–2 tablespoons sugar (optional)
1 1/2 cups cake flour, sifted
2 cups full-cream milk or buttermilk (or make a mix of 1/2 iced water and 1/2 milk)
2 tablespoons melted butter or sunflower oil

For frying:
unsalted butter

For serving:
apricot or berry jam, cinnamon sugar, lemon wedges

Blend or beat together all the batter ingredients until smooth. Allow to stand for at least half an hour. Heat a knob of butter in a pan – nonstick ensures good results and anything from 20cm–23cm in diameter is a good size. When butter is starting to brown, add a ladle of batter. Swirl around to cover the bottom of the pan, lifting if necessary to allow the excess batter to run underneath. Once nicely browned, flip to brown the other side.
Makes about 12

CHAPTER THREE

food for friends

We love to have friends from Cape Town for Sunday lunch
to share the excellent local seafood. There's plenty of crayfish in
summer, mussels for the picking and oysters to be ordered from the
nearby farm. Smoked snoek and angel fish are sold at the
St Helena Bay harbour. Bunches of shimmering small fish, perfect
for fish soup and freshly caught by local fishermen, may be bought
at the side of the road. Otherwise Paternoster does not boast
a big catch, and for fresh fish I shop in Langebaan.
In winter slow-cooked lamb, hearty and flavoursome, is the dish for
a cold day. Or even a barbecue in the courtyard, if the weather's its
usual sunny self. There's always fruit to finish, and ice-cream in
cones to enjoy on the beach. Should the weather turn stormy,
I bake a warm pudding for a special winter treat.

Crayfish is abundant and mussels are plentiful for the picking, and oysters are farmed nearby too. I buy in a box, then show friends how to shuck their own. They're more fun to eat that way, with a squeeze of lemon juice and a grinding of black pepper.

Split steamed crayfish with lemon during the season is our staple diet – and a heavenly treat for our town guests.

a crayfish killing

Professional chefs plunge the point of a sharp heavy knife into the head between the eyes, which kills them instantly. But if you're not so brave, drown them in a big bucket of cold fresh water. Weight down the lid to keep them in place. Jeffrey Steingarten, the brilliant American food writer, says that simply freezing them is kindest of all. We use sea water for cooking, not too much, in a large pot. Alternatively, flavour the water with onion, celery, parsley, thyme, peppercorns and a good bit of salt. Add the whole crayfish to the boiling water and simmer briskly for 10 minutes for medium-sized, half the time for small ones and 15 minutes for large. Take care not to overcook; the flesh should be opaque but deliciously moist. Remove with tongs and drain in a colander. Once the crayfish are cool enough to handle, split them in half lengthwise, discarding the small sand sac in the head and the intestinal tube. The coral roe and greenish-yellow tomalley are delicious, but if you don't like the look of them, carefully rinse them out. Serve with wedges of lemon and plenty of homemade lemony mayonnaise (see page 20).
Allow 1–2 halves per person

barbecued crayfish

My son's friend from Montauk, a seaside resort at the end of Long Island, taught us to cook the whole crayfish over hot coals. They slowly steam inside the shell without drying out. For a deliciously char-grilled flavour, you can also place the halved cooked crayfish, flesh-side down, on the grid over the coals to quickly brown and catch slightly.

steamed mussels with wine and herbs

This is a very basic way of preparing mussels, and still one of the best ways of eating them. It makes a good start to a barbecue, as the pot can be placed on the fire while it is still high, then enjoyed as the wood burns down to the right temperature to cook the main course.

2 kg tightly closed mussels
2 cups white wine
1/4 cup chopped Italian parsley
1/4 cup chopped celery
3 cloves garlic, crushed
1/4 cup cream (optional)
milled black pepper

STEP 1. To clean, first soak the mussels in fresh water for about an hour.

STEP 2. Then scrape the shells and pull out the beards. If any are open, tap sharply on a hard surface to see if they'll close. If not, discard.

STEP 3. Place mussels in a large, heavy saucepan with the wine, parsley, celery and garlic. Cover and heat (over the fire or on the stove) for 3 minutes, shaking now and again. Remove the mussels with tongs as they open. Give the closed ones a chance, but discard any that refuse to open. If using cream, stir into the mussel liquor and reduce slightly over a high heat. Add a grinding of black pepper and check seasoning. Return mussels to the sauce. Serve in bowls with bread for dunking. To turn into a main course, serve Belgian-style, with a bowl of thick mayonnaise and lots of crisp slim fries.
For 6 as a starter, 4 as a main course

creamy mussel risotto

1 cup dry white wine
4 cups fish stock (see page 80)
1,5 kg cleaned mussels
2 tablespoons unsalted butter
1 tablespoon olive oil
1 small onion, finely chopped
sea salt and milled black pepper
1 fat clove garlic, crushed
2 cups risotto rice
1 cup cream
chopped parsley

In a wide saucepan, heat the wine and stock. Add the cleaned mussels, remembering to discard any that aren't tightly closed. Simmer for a few minutes, just until they open. Remove with a slotted spoon as they open. Strain the stock and set aside the mussels. In a wide pan, heat the butter and oil. Stir in the onion and a pinch of salt. Cook gently until softened but still pale. Stir in the garlic, then the rice. Stir in a ladleful of the reserved stock and stir until absorbed. Keep repeating this until all the stock has been used and the rice is tender but has the required bite. If necessary, add a little more stock. It should take about 25 minutes. Heat the cream with the reserved mussels, then pour over the risotto. Check seasoning, sprinkle with parsley and serve immediately.
For 4

roast garlic prawns

If you like your prawns spicy, mix a teaspoon or so of crushed chillies with the oil – or you could use smoked Spanish paprika. I think prawns are best enjoyed shell-on, with nothing on the side besides napkins for wiping greasy hands. And perhaps some bread for dunking into the flavoured oil...

2 kg large prawns, unshelled but deveined
1 cup olive oil
6–8 fat cloves garlic, crushed
1/4–1/2 cup chopped Italian parsley

Turn the prawns onto a large baking tray. Moisten with olive oil, then spread out to form a single layer. Roast, one shelf above the middle, at 230°C for 5 minutes. Strew the garlic and parsley over the prawns and roast for another 3 minutes until pink and curled.
For 6–8

portuguese-style seafood rice

olive oil
250g prawns with shells
250g baby calamari tubes or sliced calamari
1 spicy chorizo sausage, chopped
1 onion, skinned and chopped
2 cups risotto rice
400g can chopped tomatoes
2–3 cloves garlic, crushed
good pinch saffron
1/2 cup dry white wine
2 1/2 cups fish or chicken broth
500g cleaned, tightly closed mussels
chopped parsley
sea salt and milled black pepper
fresh coriander leaves

Heat a little oil in a large heavy saucepan. Add the prawns and stir-fry briskly until pink and curled. Remove. Add the calamari and stir-fry briskly, then add the chorizo and stir-fry until browned. Remove. Add more oil and the onion. Cook gently until softened. Stir in the rice, keep stirring for a few minutes, then add the tomatoes, garlic and saffron and simmer for a few minutes. Pour in the wine and broth. Bring to a bubble, then reduce the heat, cover and cook gently for about half an hour or until the rice is swollen and tender. Add the mussels and a sprinkling of parsley. Cover and cook for about 5 minutes or until the mussels have opened (reject any that don't). If necessary, add more broth. Check seasoning. Sprinkle with more chopped parsley and fresh coriander, and serve.
For 6

crayfish with pasta

It's a joy to have leftover crayfish to turn into a delicious pasta sauce. I remove the flesh from the shells and simmer the shells with some fish stock. Once the stock is slightly reduced, strain it. To make the sauce, mix about 1 1/2 cups stock with 1/2 cup cream, some chopped fresh dill, crushed garlic, a strip of blanched lemon peel and a squeeze of lemon juice. Reduce over a high heat until slightly thickened. Add about 1 cup diced crayfish and seasoning to taste. Mix with 250g hot cooked fresh thin pasta and serve immediately.
For 2–3

smoked snoek with pan-seared tomato salsa

This is the way I like to serve smoked snoek as a starter. Smoked angel fish is good too. Both are delicious served with buttered brown bread and this simple tomato salsa.

Sear a punnet of small tomatoes in a hot pan in a little olive oil until starting to burst and catch. Remove from the heat and place the tomatoes in a serving bowl. Chop a bunch of spring onions and mix with one chopped red chilli and a good squeeze of lemon juice. Add to the tomatoes with some extra olive oil to moisten and seasoning to taste. Sometimes I add chopped avocado, fresh coriander, extra fresh lime or lemon juice, and perhaps a drizzle of avocado oil. A few chopped pickled peppadews will give it extra zing.
For 6

hot-smoked yellowtail with celery and fennel salad

'Hot' refers to the method of smoking, not the temperature of serving. Hot-smoking cooks fish, making the flesh opaque, while cold-smoking (as in traditional smoked salmon) turns it translucent. It's pretty easy to make in a ready-to-use smoking bag, sold in supermarkets.

1kg filleted yellowtail, with skin, in 2 large pieces
sea salt and milled black pepper
olive oil
smoking bag

For the salad, mix together:
1 celery heart, thinly sliced
1 bulb fennel, thinly sliced
3–4 tablespoons best olive oil
1–2 tablespoons fresh lemon juice
sea salt and milled black pepper

Preheat the oven to 250°C. With the fish at room temperature, season lightly and moisten well with olive oil. Slip it into the smoking bag, skin-side down, making sure the perforated side of the bag is facing downwards. Close the bag tightly, folding the end over twice and pressing the corners firmly closed. Place on a baking tray on the bottom rack of the oven. Smoke for 25 minutes. Remove from the oven but allow the fish to cool to room temperature before removing from the bag. Break into chunks and serve with the salad and buttered brown bread.
For 8 as a starter, 4 as a main course

fish soup with cheese toasts

1 bunch small fresh fish, cleaned
1 onion, skinned and sliced
2 or 3 leeks, sliced
2 or 3 sticks celery, sliced
3 or 4 cloves garlic, chopped
olive oil
2 or 3 ripe red tomatoes, skinned and chopped
8 cups water
1/2 cup dry white wine
1 bay leaf
chopped parsley
1 teaspoon sea salt
a few peppercorns

Preferably, have the fish skinned and filleted by the fishmonger when you buy it, but ask to keep all the heads, bones and trimmings to make the broth. If you have bought whole fish, start by skinning and filletting them, keeping all the trimmings for the broth and setting aside the fillets of fish. To make the broth, gently soften the onion, leeks, celery and garlic in 2–3 tablespoons olive oil. Add the rest of the ingredients and bring to a boil. Simmer fairly briskly, half-covered, for about half an hour. Strain and check seasoning. If necessary, reduce over a high heat to intensify the flavour. Strain the broth again through a colander lined with a clean white disposable cleaning cloth. Reheat gently and add the fillets of fish. Poach for a few minutes until opaque and just cooked. Add the cheese toasts, sprinkle with chopped parsley and serve.

For the cheese toasts:
1 cup grated Gruyère
1/2 cup thick mayonnaise
1 fat clove garlic, crushed
milled black pepper or cayenne pepper
6 slices white country bread
butter

Mix together the cheese, mayonnaise and garlic. Add pepper to taste. Cut crusts off the bread and cut into triangles. Butter one side of each triangle of bread and place, buttered-side down, on a baking tray. Spread triangles with the cheese mixture. Bake at 230°C for 10–15 minutes or until the bread is crisp and the topping golden.
For 4–6

on the barbecue

I'm new to this game – there's no tradition of braaing in our family and the only one keen on making a fire is my son. He introduced me to the charcoal chimney and showed me how to make beer chicken, an American favourite. I usually choose one barbecued dish and do the rest on the stove or in the oven.

barbecued fish steaks with lemon and basil dressing

4 fish steaks, about 750g
sea salt and milled black peppers
olive oil

For the dressing, blend together:
1/3 cup olive oil
1/4 cup fresh lemon juice
handful of basil leaves
grated zest of 1 lemon
sea salt and milled black pepper

For serving:
hot steamed potato slices
shredded crispy lettuce

Season and oil the fish. Grill over the coals until starting to char but still moist inside. Immediately place on a pile of potato slices and lettuce, drench with dressing and serve.
For 4

beer chicken

I often use a vertical roaster in the oven, as it works like a spit-roast in reverse, allowing the skin of the chicken to crisp and brown all over. Here the chicken is balanced over a can of beer to keep it upright, and the steam from the liquid ensures a moist bird. First season the chicken, stuff it with some fresh herbs or use your favourite rub. Roast indoors at 200°C for an hour or until golden and tender. Or cook it in a kettle braai in the usual way.
For 4

barbecued boerewors rolls with basil, rocket and tomato-chilli jam

Sandwich hot barbecued boerewors in slashed panini rolls, which can be lightly toasted over the coals if you like. Add lots of basil leaves and rocket, plus a good smear of store-bought tomato-chilli jam.

grilled whole eggplants with bruschetta

1 medium eggplant per person
olive oil
fresh lemon juice
sea salt and milled black pepper

For the bruschetta:
ciabatta loaf, sliced
good olive oil
1 head garlic, halved

Prick the eggplants and grill on the barbecue until charred outside and meltingly soft inside. To make the bruschetta, brush the sliced bread with olive oil, then toast over the coals. Remove and smear with the halved head of garlic. To serve the eggplant, slash a cross on top of each one, squash the sides to open and flavour with olive oil, lemon juice and seasoning.

barbecued beef burgers

To make the burgers, knead together:
500g lean beef mince
1 chopped onion, fried
1 clove garlic, crushed
1 tablespoon capers, chopped
a few anchovy fillets, chopped
1 teaspoon Worcestershire sauce
1 beaten egg
salt and milled black pepper to taste
1 slice wholewheat bread, crumbled and soaked in 1/4 cup water

To grill the burgers:
vegetable oil

Shape the beef mixture into 4 patties. Moisten with oil and grill until nicely browned but still medium-rare. Serve with a crunchy salad of coarsely shredded crisp lettuce and red cabbage, thinly sliced red onion and radishes, and torn Italian parsley, all tossed with enough olive oil to moisten, plus lemon juice, sea salt and milled black pepper to taste.
For 4

barbecued sardines with winter slaw

Sardines come frozen, but not necessarily cleaned, so ask your fishmonger to clean and scale them. When fresh haarders are available, use them. Sometimes I serve the sardines on potatoes with bitter salad leaves, curly endive or chicory.

8–12 cleaned sardines
olive oil
coarse sea salt and black pepper
whole chives
thinly sliced fennel

For the slaw, mix together:
2 shredded white baby cabbages
2 shredded red baby cabbages
8–10 sliced radishes
1 small red onion, sliced
a torn head of radicchio or small red lettuce
2 tablespoons lemon juice
5 tablespoons olive oil
1 clove crushed garlic
1 teaspoon Dijon mustard
sea salt and milled black pepper

Moisten the sardines with oil. Season, inside and out, with coarse sea salt and black pepper. Stuff with chives and fennel. Grill over hot coals for about 5 minutes a side until crisp and just cooked through. Spoon the hot sardines onto the slaw and serve.
For 4 as a starter, 2 as a main course

To make the alternative salad of potatoes and winter greens, whisk 3 tablespoons of white wine vinegar with 1/3 cup olive oil, 3–4 chopped spring onions, 2–3 tablespoons chopped parsley and seasoning to taste to make the dressing. Mix 500g hot cooked halved small potatoes with half the dressing and turn onto a plate of bitter salad leaves, endive or chicory, then top with the just-off-the-grill sardines and spoon over the rest of the dressing.

I love to shove a big casserole into the oven to slowly cook to eat-with-a-spoon tenderness. Meanwhile I read a book or, hypnotised by the ocean, watch the waves through the window. Spoon the lamb into big open bowls for serving. All that's needed are chunks of bread for dunking, but if you like, make mash, potatoes or pulses, or hot, soft polenta. Follow with a mix of greens, lightly tossed in olive oil and wine vinegar.

slow-roasted lamb shanks

6–8 lamb shanks
olive oil
2 cups dry red wine
2 large onions, finely chopped
3–4 cloves garlic, crushed
250g ripe tomatoes, skinned and chopped
3 or 4 sprigs rosemary
1 bay leaf
strip of orange peel or dried naartjie peel
sea salt and milled black pepper
2–3 sticks celery, sliced
2–3 carrots, chopped (optional)
2 tablespoons tomato paste
1–2 cups chicken or beef stock
125g rindless streaky bacon (optional)

Pack the shanks into an oiled heavy casserole. Add the wine, onions, garlic, tomatoes, herbs, citrus peel and a good grinding of black pepper. Leave to marinate for a few hours or overnight in the fridge. Allow to return to room temperature before cooking. Add salt, celery, carrots (if using), tomato paste and enough stock to just cover the meat. Add 2 tablespoons olive oil or the bacon (if using), blanched in boiling water first. Cover with 1–2 sheets of oiled greaseproof paper and a tight-fitting lid. Bake at 120–140°C for 5–7 hours or until meat is soft enough to eat with a spoon. Remove the shanks and keep warm. Reduce the cooking liquids on top of the stove over a high heat to a rich, chunky consistency. If you prefer a smoother sauce, blend with a hand-held electric stick blender. Check seasoning. Pour over the lamb or return to the casserole to serve kitchen-style.
For 6–8

Variation: when quinces are in season, add a few to the casserole. Don't bother to peel, simply slice into thick wedges or cut in half. Leave out the tomatoes and add a cup of port, the juice of 1 or 2 lemons and a stick of cinnamon.

whole pear batter pudding

6–8 whole wine-poached pears (see page 32)
butter

For the batter, beat together:
1/4 cup sugar
1/2 cup flour
pinch salt
3 extra-large free-range eggs
1 cup milk
2 tablespoons brandy

For serving:
icing sugar, ground cinnamon (optional), crème fraîche

Arrange the pears in a buttered baking dish. Pour the batter around the pears. Bake at 180°C for about an hour or until golden. Dredge with icing sugar and, if you like, dust with cinnamon. Serve warm with crème fraîche.
For 8

baked strawberries

500g strawberries, hulled
butter
3 free-range egg yolks
1/4 cup sugar
2 tablespoons flour
1 cup full-cream milk, warmed
2 tablespoons Van der Hum liqueur
5 egg whites
icing sugar

Roughly crush the strawberries and turn into a buttered shallow ovenproof dish. Beat the egg yolks with 2 tablespoons of the sugar until thick. Beat in the flour, then the warm milk. Bring to the boil, stirring constantly. Remove from the heat and add the liqueur. Whisk the egg whites until soft peaks form, then beat in the remaining sugar and whisk until stiff. Lighten the cooked mixture with a little of the beaten egg whites, then gently fold into the rest of the egg whites. Spoon over the strawberries and bake at 200°C for 10 minutes or until puffed and golden. Sift icing sugar over and bake for another 5 minutes.
For 6

cinnamon ice cream with cinnamon phyllo sticks

2 cups double cream
1 vanilla pod, split lengthwise
4 cinnamon sticks
8 egg yolks
1 cup caster sugar
pinch of salt
2 cups whipping cream

For the cinnamon phyllo sticks:
1 sheet phyllo pastry, melted butter, caster sugar, ground cinnamon

Pour the double cream into a saucepan. Add vanilla pod and 3 cinnamon sticks. Bring just to the boil, then remove from the heat and leave to infuse for an hour. Beat egg yolks, sugar and salt together until pale and creamy. Gradually beat in the strained infused cream. Scrape the vanilla seeds from the pod and add. Grind the remaining dry stick of cinnamon in a spice grinder or clean coffee grinder to a fine powder and add, or add 1 teaspoon store-bought ground cinnamon. Heat through gently, stirring, until a whiff of steam rises, but do not allow to boil. Pour into a bowl and allow to cool. Whip the remaining 2 cups cream and fold into the cooled custard. Freeze in an ice-cream machine according to instructions. Alternatively, turn into a freezeproof container and freeze, whisking every half hour to break up the ice crystals and ensure a creamy texture.

To make the cinnamon phyllo sticks, brush a sheet of phyllo with melted butter. Sprinkle with sugar and cinnamon. Cut into small rectangles, the length of a cinnamon stick. Roll up to resemble curled cinnamon sticks. Bake at 190°C until golden brown, dust generously with cinnamon and serve with the cinnamon ice cream.
For 8–10

mango ice cream

4 free-range egg yolks
1/2 cup caster sugar
pinch of salt
1 cup cream, warmed
1 cup sieved, puréed mango
1 tablespoon rum
1 cup whipped cream

For serving:
fresh mint, chopped fresh mango and chopped ginger preserve (optional)

Beat egg yolks with sugar and salt. Gradually beat in warmed cream. Return to the stove and heat through, stirring, until slightly thickened. Take care not to let it boil. Pour into a bowl and place a piece of greaseproof paper directly on the surface. Allow to cool, then fold in the puréed mango, rum and whipped cream. Turn into 4–6 ramekins, cover and freeze until firm. Garnish with mint, mango and chopped ginger preserve.
For 4–6

tea and sundowners

I like to invite the locals for tea, then to stay
for a drink and something savoury as the sun goes down.
I rarely have time to bake in the city, and baking is fun to do
at leisure. There's something so satisfying about turning out
a perfect cake, whether a light sponge or a dark, dense chocolate cake.
Or admiring scones, nicely risen, cooling on a wire rack.
Split and spread with thick cream and a berry jam, they're
a favourite tea-time treat. No-one can resist an iced cupcake—pastel and
pretty, they're the kind of kids' stuff that grown-ups never tire of.
By the time the sun sets, it's definitely necessary to shake a cocktail, or
pour the bubbly, and pass around some nice nibbles.
Homeroasted nuts, lemony olives, or a sharp pickle. And I love small
sandwiches too, anything from prawn mayonnaise
to sweet onion and rocket.

buttermilk scones

2 cups flour
1 tablespoon baking powder
pinch salt
100g cold unsalted butter
1 free-range egg
1/2 cup buttermilk
beaten egg or milk

For serving:
thick cream, strawberry or cherry preserves

Sift the flour, baking powder and salt together. Grate in the cold butter and rub lightly together with fingertips. Beat the egg with the buttermilk, then stir into the flour-butter mixture. Lightly knead together, then pat out thickly on a floured board. Cut out rounds and place on a floured baking sheet. Lightly knead the remaining dough and repeat. Brush the top of each one with beaten egg or milk. Bake at 220°C, one shelf above the middle, for 10 minutes or until well-risen and golden. Cool on a wire rack, but serve as fresh as possible. To serve, split open, spread with thick cream and top with preserves.
Makes 8

white fruitcake with sugar crust

250g fruitcake mix
2–3 tablespoons brandy
1/2 cup sugar cubes
grated rind of 2 large bright lemons
2–3 tablespoons melted butter
3 cups flour
4 teaspoons baking powder
1 teaspoon salt
250g unsalted butter, at room temperature
2 cups caster sugar
4 free-range eggs
1 cup full-cream milk
1 teaspoon vanilla extract

Place the fruitcake mix in a bowl. Pour over boiling water, then drain. Cover with brandy and leave to steep while preparing the tin and making the batter. Coat a tube cake tin very well with nonstick cooking spray. Roughly crush the sugar cubes, mix together with the lemon rind and melted butter and spoon into the bottom of the prepared tin. Sift the flour, baking powder and salt together. Using an electric mixer, cream the butter and sugar until light and fluffy. Beat in the eggs, one at a time. At low speed, fold in the sifted flour mixture, alternately with the milk, beginning and ending with flour. Stir in the vanilla extract. Fold in the brandied fruits by hand. Spoon the batter into the tin and smooth the top. Bake at 190°C, one shelf below the centre, for about an hour or until a tester inserted comes out clean. Allow to stand for 10 minutes before inverting onto a wire rack to cool completely. If the sugar crust sticks to the bottom of the pan, carefully remove it and pat onto the top of the cake. Or, if you prefer, leave out the sugar crust altogether and simply dust the plain cake with sifted icing sugar.
For 12

lemon-curd roll

4 eggs
1 cup sugar
1 cup cake flour
1 teaspoon baking powder
pinch salt

STEP 1. Beat the eggs with the sugar until very light and fluffy.

STEP 2. Sift the flour with the baking powder and salt, then sift over the beaten mixture and fold in gently but evenly.

STEP 3. Turn into a buttered baking swiss-roll pan lined with nonstick baking paper. Bake, one shelf above the middle, at 200°C for about 12 minutes or until nicely risen.

STEP 4. Turn out and pull off the paper carefully. Place a clean sheet of baking paper on top, then roll up, lengthwise, in a tea towel.

For the lemon-curd filling:
3 farm or 2 extra-large free-range eggs
2 egg yolks
1/2 cup caster sugar
1/2 cup strained lemon juice
grated rind of 2 lemons
125g chilled unsalted butter

Beat the whole eggs and yolks until frothy, then gradually beat in the sugar until thick and pale. Mix in the lemon juice and rind. Turn into a heavy saucepan and cook over a medium heat, whisking in the butter bit by bit. Cook for about 5 minutes, until thickened, but take care not to allow it to boil and curdle. Once thickened, remove from the stove and place a piece of nonstick paper directly on the surface. Leave to cool completely. Refrigerate for a few hours until it is a good spreading consistency.

STEP 5. To assemble the cake, carefully unroll the sponge cake, spread with the lemon-curd filling and roll up again.
For 8

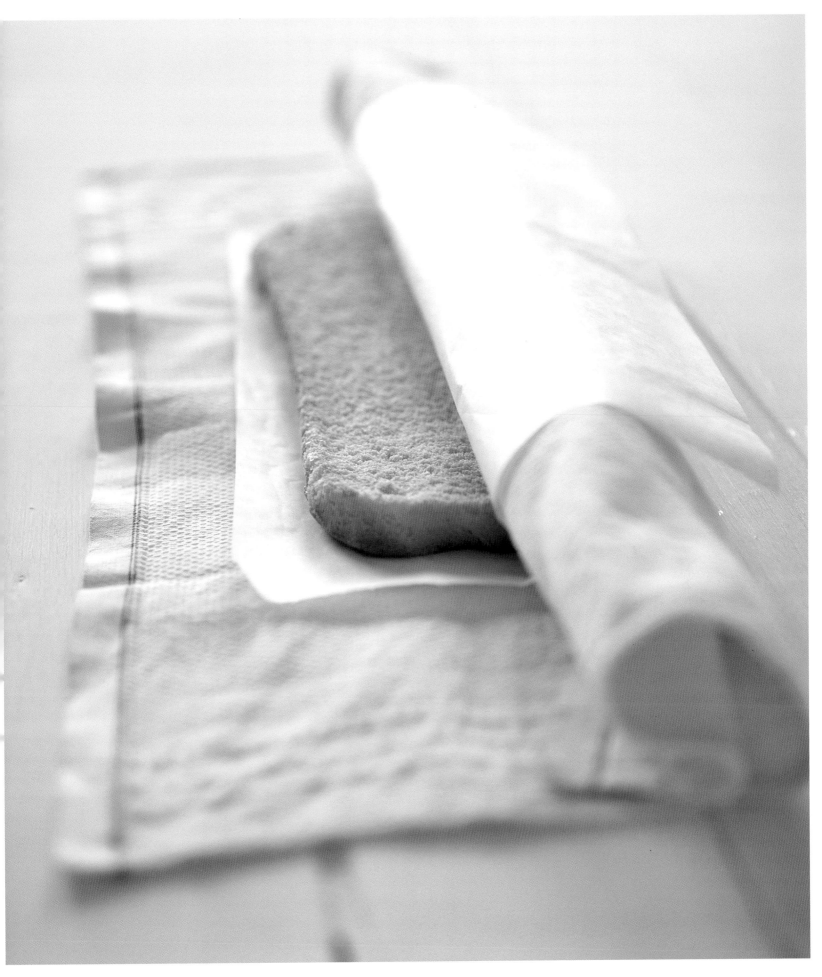

iced cupcakes

1/2 cup full-cream milk
1 tablespoon butter
1 cup sifted flour
1 teaspoon baking powder
pinch salt
3 free-range eggs
1 cup sugar
2 teaspoons vanilla extract*

For decorating:
fresh-cream icing, sugar flowers (optional)

Heat the milk until bubbles form around the edge of the pan. Remove from heat and stir in the butter. Allow to cool. Sift the flour with the baking powder and salt. Using an electric mixer, beat the eggs until pale. Gradually beat in the sugar until thick and creamy. At low speed, blend in flour mixture until just smooth. Add still-warm milk and vanilla. Beat until just combined. Line large muffin pans with paper cookie cases. Ladle batter into each one and bake at 200°C in the centre of the oven for 15 minutes or until golden and firm to the touch. A tester inserted should come out clean. Allow to cool before icing.

To make the fresh-cream icing:
1 1/2 cups sifted icing sugar
1/3 cup fresh cream

Mix the icing sugar with enough cream to make a good spreading consistency.

To assemble the cupcakes, coat each one with icing and, if you like, top with a sugar flower.
Makes 12

***Note:** to make your own vanilla flavouring, pound or process 1 chopped vanilla pod with 2 tablespoons brandy. Store in a small bottle and strain before using.

mixed berry tartlets

For the pastry:
1 1/2 cups cake flour
2 tablespoons icing sugar
pinch salt
100g chilled unsalted butter
1 tablespoon sunflower oil
1 free-range egg yolk
1 tablespoon sweet sherry
1 tablespoon iced water

Sift together the flour, icing sugar and salt. Cut in the butter and rub lightly with the fingertips to form coarse crumbs. Whisk together the oil, egg yolk, sherry and iced water. Stir into the flour mixture until moistened. Knead lightly to form a dough. Wrap well and chill for about half an hour. Divide the dough in half. Pat the one half into a rectangle on a sheet of nonstick baking paper. Cover with a second sheet of nonstick baking paper and roll out thinly. Stamp out small rounds using a 5cm pastry cutter. Press down into small muffin pans. Prick well and freeze while heating the oven to 200°C. Bake for 10–12 minutes or until golden brown and crisp. Allow to cool.

For the filling:
1/2 cup redcurrant jelly
1 tablespoon brandy or Kirsch
500g fresh mixed berries

Melt the jelly with the brandy. Mix together with the fresh berries and use to fill the tart shells.
Makes 12–18

fresh fig tart

For the pastry:
Make the same pastry given in the recipe for berry tartlets (see page 106), but roll it out to fit a 22,5cm loose-bottomed tart tin and prick well. Cover with plastic wrap and refrigerate or freeze while heating the oven to 200°C. Bake blind for 10 minutes or until set but not browned. Allow to cool.

For the filling:
about 12 ripe fresh figs
2 free-range egg yolks
1/2 cup fresh cream
2 tablespoons runny honey
1 tablespoon brandy
icing sugar

Peel the figs and cut each one across, almost right through. Arrange in the bottom of the cooled tart shell. Beat the egg yolks, cream, honey and brandy together and pour over the figs. Bake at 180°C for 20 minutes. Remove from the oven, sift icing sugar over, then bake for another 10 minutes or until set. Allow to cool slightly before removing from the tin.
For 6–8

open apple pie

8–10 apples
squeeze of lemon juice
butter
brown sugar
honey
nutmeg
cinnamon sticks
handful of seedless raisins, soaked in boiling water
1 cup apple cider
1 sheet puff pastry
beaten egg

For serving:
crème fraîche or thick sour cream

Peel the apples, dropping them into a basin of water flavoured with the lemon juice. Slice into thick wedges, discarding the seeds and cores. Arrange on a well-buttered baking tray. Sprinkle with sugar, drizzle with honey and dot with butter. Add a grating of nutmeg and tuck in some cinnamon sticks. Sprinkle with the drained raisins. Pour over some cider – a cup should be enough. Bake at 200°C for 40 minutes or until starting to get soft. Top with cut-out puff-pastry shapes (I rather like hearts). Remove from the oven, brush pastry shapes with beaten egg and return to the oven for about 20 minutes or until the pastry is puffed and golden and the apples are tender. Serve with crème fraîche or thick sour cream.
For 6–8

lavender shortbread

For the shortbread:
2 cups cake flour
1/4 cup cornflour
pinch salt
2/3 cup caster sugar
250g unsalted butter
unsprayed lavender flowers

For serving:
icing sugar, lavender flowers

Sift together flour, cornflour and salt. Stir in caster sugar and cut in the butter. Rub lightly together with the fingertips until it forms a dough. Press into two 15–18 cm loose-bottomed tart tins. Cut each one into wedges and prick neatly. Press in lavender flowers. Freeze while heating the oven to 160°C. Bake for 45 minutes or until pale brown. Cut into wedges again and allow to cool. Sift icing sugar over and strew with lavender flowers.
For 8

old-fashioned creamy fudge

I do find all the stirring a bit of a bore, but the lure of proper fudge, the melt-in-the-mouth kind, motivates me, especially on a wet Saturday with the fire crackling.

4 cups sugar
1 cup full-cream milk
2 tablespoons golden syrup
125g butter, cut into pieces
pinch salt
1 tin condensed milk
pinch cream of tartar
1 teaspoon vanilla extract

Place the sugar, milk, syrup, butter and salt in a large, heavy saucepan. Stir over a fierce heat until the butter melts. Bring to a boil and allow to boil for 5 minutes. Reduce heat and stir in the condensed milk and cream of tartar. Stirring all the time without fail, boil the mixture for 20 to 25 minutes until, when tested in cold water, a small ball holds its shape. By this time the saucepan will be sugary round the sides. Remove from heat and beat in the vanilla. Pour into a well-buttered pan and allow to cool. When set, cut into squares.
Makes about 1 kg

real chocolate cake

Now this delicious recipe comes from a superb food magazine, Cook's Illustrated, an American publication. It's not glossy and gorgeous, but serious about food. Dedicated to excellence, the team of test cooks work nonstop until they come up with the best recipe: 130 cakes were baked before David Pazmino was satisfied that this was the perfect old-fashioned American chocolate layer cake. He sandwiches and ices it with an awesome rich, creamy and buttery frosting. But for afternoon tea in the country, I simply bake it in one deep tin and quickly glaze it. I also quite like the German indulgence of topping a wedge of chocolate cake with a cloud of softly whipped cream.

100g dark chocolate, broken into bits
1/4 cup cocoa
1/2 cup hot water
1 3/4 cups sugar
1 3/4 cups flour
1 1/2 teaspoons bicarbonate of soda
1 teaspoon salt
4 extra-large free-range eggs
2 egg yolks
175g unsalted butter, softened
1 cup buttermilk
2 teaspoons vanilla extract

Place chocolate, cocoa and hot water in a heatproof bowl over simmering water, stirring until the chocolate melts. Add 1/2 cup sugar and keep stirring for a minute or two until glossy. Set aside to cool. Sift the flour, bicarbonate of soda and salt together. In a large bowl, using an electric mixer, whisk the eggs and yolks together. Gradually whisk in the remaining 1 1/4 cups sugar and beat relentlessly until pale and fluffy. Beat in the cooled chocolate. Gradually beat in the softened butter, a tablespoon at a time, until thick and creamy. At low speed beat in the flour mixture alternately with the buttermilk, beginning and ending with the flour. Fold in the vanilla with a spatula and check to see that all the flour is properly incorporated.
Turn into a 23cm springform cake tin coated with a nonstick cooking spray and lined with a circle of baking paper. Bake at 180°C for 40 minutes or until a tester inserted comes out clean. Cool for about 15 minutes before removing from the tin. Allow to cool to room temperature before glazing.

For the glaze:
100g dark chocolate, 3–4 tablespoons fresh cream
Melt the chocolate and the cream together. Pour or spread over the cake.

mushroom crostini

400g mushrooms, finely chopped
2–3 tablespoons olive oil
2–3 tablespoons chopped Italian parsley
1 clove garlic, crushed
1 tablespoon balsamic vinegar
sea salt and milled black pepper
3 or more chopped anchovies
panini or baguette, sliced

Stir-fry the mushrooms in the olive oil over a high heat until all the liquid has evaporated. Mix with the rest of the ingredients. To make the crostini: toast thin slices of panini or baguette at 200°C for 5–10 minutes until golden. Spoon the mushroom mixture onto the crostini and serve immediately.
For 6

roasted nuts

Roast a mix of nuts–almonds, raw cashews, macadamias–at 160°C for 10 minutes or until golden brown. Season with coarse sea salt and add a twist of black pepper or paprika if you like. If you like them spicy, add a sprinkling of chilli powder, some cumin and coriander, or simply some garam masala.

chicken-liver confit

For me this confit is even more delicious than a regular pâté. Lovely on warm crusty bread, on hot toast, or spread on crisp crostini.

500g free-range chicken livers
2 or 3 garlic cloves, smashed
a few sprigs thyme
sea salt and milled black pepper
olive oil

Place the trimmed, cleaned chicken livers in a saucepan just large enough to take them in a single layer. Add garlic, thyme and seasoning. Barely cover with olive oil – about 2/3 cup should do. Cover with a snug-fitting lid and cook on the lowest possible heat for about 25 minutes or until firm to the touch. Lift out the livers and place in a suitable container, then strain over the oil. Push down the livers so that they are immersed and, if necessary, add a little more oil. Store in the refrigerator.
For 8

lemony garlic olives

1 jar olives, green or black
2 lemons
a few garlic cloves, smashed
olive oil

Drain and rinse the olives. Turn into a bowl. Add the pulp and juice of the 2 lemons and the garlic. Cover with oil. Allow to stand at room temperature for an hour or two before serving, but for storing, keep covered in the fridge.
For 6–8

quick dill pickles

18–24 small crisp cucumbers
24 peppercorns
10 bay leaves
4 cloves garlic, smashed
handful of fresh dill sprigs
1 cup white wine vinegar
2 1/2 cups water
2 tablespoons sugar
1 tablespoon salt

Scrub the cucumbers but leave whole. Place in a jar with the peppercorns, bay leaves, garlic and dill. Bring the vinegar, water, sugar and salt to the boil and simmer for a few minutes. Remove from the heat. Allow to cool, and when cold, pour over the cucumbers. Refrigerate overnight – or all day – before using, but they keep well for at least a week.
Makes 1 jar

eggplant hummus

about 600g eggplant
2 cloves garlic, crushed
1/2 cup tahini
sea salt and milled black pepper
1/3 cup lemon juice
1 teaspoon ground cumin
1 can chickpeas, drained
pinch cayenne pepper

Prick and grill the eggplants until blackened, then bake at 230°C for 15 minutes or until very soft. Allow to cool. Remove the flesh from the skins, then blend with the remaining ingredients until smooth.
For 6–8

prawn mayo sandwiches

20 thin slices soft white bread

For the filling:
250g frozen cooked and peeled cocktail prawns
squeeze of lemon juice
3–4 tablespoons thick mayonnaise
sea salt and milled black pepper

It's easiest to buy a ready-sliced loaf for these, or have it sliced at the store. Defrost the prawns overnight in the fridge, in a colander over a bowl to catch the liquid. Pat dry with paper towel and mix with the lemon juice and mayonnaise. Check seasoning. Cut the bread into squares, discarding the crusts. Sandwich with the prawn filling. Leave as squares or cut into fingers.
Makes 10–20

wild rocket and sweet onion sandwiches

Onion sandwiches were one of mid-twentieth-century American food writer James Beard's favourite cocktail items – genteel circles of soft white bread, well-buttered, sandwiched with sweet onion, then the edges rolled in mayonnaise and chopped parsley. Too fiddly for me. But now that sweet onions are available, I do make this simpler rendition.

thinly sliced white sandwich loaf
thick mayonnaise
thinly sliced sweet onions
wild rocket
sea salt and milled black pepper

Trim the crusts from the bread and cut into triangles. Spread with thick mayonnaise and sandwich with onion slices, rocket and seasoning.

gruyère cheese puffs

90g unsalted butter, cut into bits
1 cup water
pinch salt
milled black pepper
1 1/3 cups flour, sifted
5 large free-range eggs
2 cups coarsely grated Gruyère

Place the butter in a small saucepan. Add the water and salt. Bring to the boil, then remove from the heat and, using a wooden spoon, stir in the pepper and flour. Return to a medium heat and cook, stirring, for a minute or so until thickened. Take off the stove again and briskly stir in the eggs, one at a time and still using the wooden spoon, until well combined. Stir in about three-quarters of the cheese. Drop heaped tablespoons, well spaced, onto a baking sheet lined with nonstick baking paper. Sprinkle with the rest of the cheese. Bake at 200°C for 20 minutes or until puffed and golden. Cool on a wire rack but serve while warm.
Makes about 24–30

deep-fried whitebait with lemon

Whitebait are tiny silver fish that are delicious eaten whole, deep-fried until golden and crispy.

500g whole whitebait
flour
sunflower oil
lemon wedges

You'll usually find whitebait frozen, but don't bother to defrost as the fish are so tiny; simply rinse and pat dry. Dust with flour and deep-fry in hot oil until golden brown. Drain on paper towel and serve with lemon wedges.
For 4

homemade lemonade and gin fizz

For the lemonade:
6 juicy lemons
1 cup boiling water
2 cups sugar
pinch salt

For the cocktails:
gin
lots of ice
lemon slices
mint leaves
sparkling mineral water or soda water

For the lemonade, pour boiling water over the lemons. Using a zester, scrape thin strips from 2 of the lemons. Place zest in a saucepan with the sugar, water and salt. Stir until the sugar has dissolved, then boil for 5 minutes. Cool and add the juice of all 6 lemons. Strain and refrigerate in a sealed jar.

To make the cocktails, use 2 tablespoons syrup to 2 tablespoons gin for each one. Add lots of ice, mint leaves and a twist of lemon. Top up with sparkling mineral water or soda water.
Makes about 3 cups, enough for about 20 cocktails.

watermelon cocktails

2 tablespoons sugar
1/2 cup cold water
5 or 6 ice cubes
2 cups watermelon chunks, seeded (or any other melon)

Blend all the ingredients until smooth. Serve well chilled, or over ice, adding a generous slug of tequila or white rum.
For 3–4

CHAPTER FIVE

out and about

It's fun to go on excursions. A drive through dairy farms to
St Helena Bay. There's a memorial to Vasco da Gama, the
Portuguese navigator who first visited the West Coast in the 17th
century. Or a visit to Velddrif, home to the salt pans, for a beer at the
hotel on the harbour. I love the boat trip along the Berg River
to see the flamingos at sunset. Further up the coast is
Muisbosskerm, an outdoor eatery on the beach that is
renowned for its traditional West Coast braai.
The village of Redelinghuys in the Verlorenvlei area, one of the
largest wetlands on the West Coast, boasts the best potatoes in the
Sandveld region. It also produces heerbone, a prized variety
of bean that is not well-known today, but at one time was exported
to Buckingham Palace. This is the bean that I buy at the farm stall
near Vredenburg. And Kersefontein honey, from the hives
on the banks of the Berg River, is rapidly establishing a
reputation for its unique flavour and fragrance.

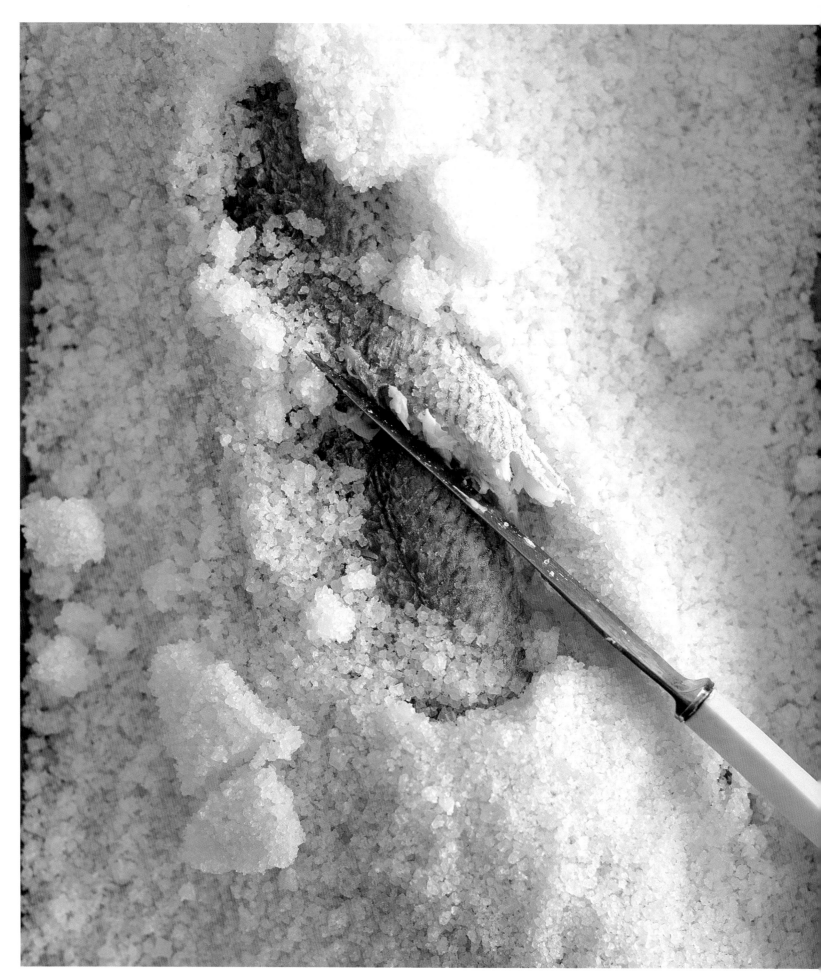

salt-baked fish

With all the salt around the corner, it seemed a good idea to bury a fish in it, then bake until just cooked and still moist. The best way to enhance the gentle flavour is with a simple squeeze of lemon. The simplicity of the dish demands the freshest of fish.

2–3 kg coarse salt
1 whole firm-fleshed fish, 750g–1 kg, cleaned

For serving:
wild rocket
lemon wedges
olive oil
milled black pepper

Turn half the salt into an ovenproof pan that will take the fish snugly. Spread the salt to form a fairly even layer. Place the fish on top and cover with the remaining salt. Bake at 220°C for half an hour until the salt feels firm to the touch. Crack the crust to get to the fish. Remove the skin and all the salt. Serve the filleted fish with wild rocket and lemon wedges for squeezing. Drizzle with olive oil and add a twist or two of black pepper.
For 2–3

Along the banks of the Berg River in Velddrif you'll see racks of bunched small fish — haarders, salted and drying in the sun. It's a traditional method of preserving, resulting in a kind of fish biltong called bokkoms. The salty fillets are eaten with sweet grapes, and they're also good with thickly buttered fresh bread and a dab of grape jam. They are a true regional speciality.

cold baked fish with lemon-dill sauce

1 whole firm-fleshed fish, about 1,5kg, divided into 2 large fillets
olive or sunflower oil
1 onion, thinly sliced
1/3 cup strained lemon juice
sea salt and milled black pepper

For the sauce, mix together:
2 cups thick mayonnaise
1 cup buttermilk
2 tablespoons chopped dill
1 tablespoon lemon juice
1 crushed clove garlic
sea salt and milled black pepper

For garnishing:
fresh dill, lemon wedges

Arrange the fillets of fish in an oiled baking tin just large enough to take them snugly. Tuck onion slices underneath and pour over the lemon juice. Season and drizzle with oil. Cover with oiled greaseproof paper and bake at 190°C for 20–30 minutes or until just cooked, moist, opaque and firm to the touch. Allow to cool and remove any skin. Break up into fairly large chunks and turn onto a platter. Pour over the sauce and chill for a few hours. Sprinkle with torn sprigs of fresh dill. Serve with a bowl of salad greens and hot baby potatoes, lightly tossed in good olive oil and seasoning. At the table, pass around the rest of the sauce and some lemon wedges for squeezing over the fish.
For 6

smoked mussel, roasted fennel and potato salad

200g smoked mussels
2–4 fennel bulbs
4 medium baking potatoes
olive oil
sea salt and milled black pepper
200g washed baby-leaf greens
1 cos lettuce, washed, dried and sliced

For the dressing, mix together:
2 tablespoons lemon juice
1 tablespoon balsamic vinegar
1 clove garlic, crushed
1/3 cup olive oil
sea salt and milled black pepper

For serving:
fennel fronds

Make the dressing and pour it over the smoked mussels. Leave to marinate for an hour in the refrigerator. Cut the trimmed fennel bulbs and scrubbed potatoes into wedges. Moisten with olive oil, season lightly and roast at 220°C for 20–30 minutes or until tender. Toss the marinated mussels with the fennel, potatoes and salad greens. Check seasoning. Garnish with snipped fennel fronds and serve.
For 4

When cooking for a crowd, it's easier to buy the local farmed mussels than try to pick large enough quantities off the rocks. I often simply steam them with wine and herbs (see page 72) but I also enjoy making this hearty soup.

mussel and coriander soup

1,5 kg mussels
1 1/2 cups dry white wine
1 bay leaf
3 tablespoons olive oil
1 large onion, chopped
2 cloves garlic, crushed
3 x 400g cans tomatoes in juice, crushed
pinch sugar
3 cups hot fish stock
pinch saffron
strip of orange peel
1/4 cup chopped coriander leaves
sea salt and milled black pepper

For serving:
thin cream, fresh coriander leaves

Place the scrubbed, cleaned, tightly-closed mussels in a saucepan with the wine and bay leaf. Cook over a high heat, covered, for a few minutes until the mussels open. (Discard those that don't.) Strain the liquor and reserve along with the mussels. In the heated oil, gently soften the onion. Stir in the garlic, then add the tomatoes and sugar and cook, uncovered, stirring now and again, for 10–15 minutes. Pour in the reserved mussel liquor, the hot fish stock, saffron and orange peel. Cook, partially covered, for about 20 minutes. Remove the peel and purée the soup. Add the chopped coriander leaves and check seasoning. Leave some mussels in the shell for garnishing, but shell the rest. Add to the soup, slicing them if large. Check seasoning. Serve hot, or well-chilled, drizzled with a little cream and sprinkled with fresh coriander.
For 8

roasted herb-stuffed fish steaks

4 thick firm white fish fillets, about 250g each
olive oil
1 cup chopped fresh herbs (a mix of Italian parsley, basil and lemon thyme)
2–3 cloves garlic, chopped
2 tablespoons butter
sea salt and milled pepper
lemons

Moisten the fish with olive oil and season. Mix the herbs with the garlic, butter and a little seasoning. Cut slashes into the fillets and stuff the garlic-and-herb butter into the slashes. Place, skin-side down, on an oiled baking tray. Roast at a fierce 250°C for 7–10 minutes or until just cooked and still wonderfully moist. Serve with lemon quarters for squeezing over the fish. Some kind of potato accompaniment would be good too, either steamed and soft or crisp and crusty.
For 4

angel-fish pâté

250g smoked angel fish, deboned, skinned and flaked
1/4 cup thick cream
1/4 cup farm butter, at room temperature
good squeeze of lemon juice
sea salt and milled black pepper

Blend or process the ingredients together until smooth.
For 6

fish and feta pie

750g kingklip, skinned, filleted and sliced
1/2 cup dry white wine
1 bay leaf
a few peppercorns
a few sprigs dill
salt
125g smoked angel fish or smoked salmon trout

For the sauce:
2 tablespoons butter
2 tablespoons flour
cooking liquid from the fish
1 cup full-cream milk, warmed
2 tablespoons chopped fresh dill
100g feta, crumbled
sea salt and milled black pepper

For the mashed-potato topping:
750g potatoes, peeled and cubed
1/4 cup cream
1/4 cup full-cream milk
60g butter
sea salt and milled black pepper

To assemble the pie:
grated nutmeg

To prepare the fish, gently poach the sliced kingklip in the wine with the bay leaf, peppercorns, dill and a little salt for 5 minutes or until just cooked. Strain but reserve 1/2 cup of the cooking liquid. Separate into large flakes and mix with the flaked smoked fish.

To make the sauce, melt the butter in a small heavy saucepan. Whisk in the flour until smooth. Remove from the heat and gradually whisk in the strained reserved cooking liquid and warmed milk until smooth and thickened. Remove from the heat and stir in the dill and feta. Check seasoning.

To make the potato topping, steam the potatoes until tender. Drain off the water, then add the cream and milk and cut in the butter. Heat through, then turn into a large deep bowl and mash together. Finally, whisk with an electric balloon whisk (I use the attachment to my hand-held electric stick blender) until fluffy. Check seasoning.

To assemble the pie, mix the sauce with the fish and turn into a buttered baking dish. Top with the mashed potato and sprinkle with nutmeg. Bake at 200°C for about 30 minutes or until piping hot and golden. Good with some wilted spinach leaves on the side.
For 4–6

baked sweet potatoes with orange-coriander butter

6 sweet potatoes

For the orange-coriander butter, pound together:
100g farm butter, at room temperature
zest of 1 orange
1/4 cup chopped coriander leaves
1 clove garlic, crushed
1 chilli, chopped (optional)
sea salt and milled black pepper

Scrub and prick the sweet potatoes. Bake in the oven or wrap in foil and bake buried in the coals until soft enough to eat. Slash the tops and squeeze the sides. Add a big spoonful of the flavoured butter and serve.
For 6

baby potato salad

750g baby potatoes, well-scrubbed but not peeled
a few sprigs thyme
1/4 cup apple-cider vinegar
1 cup thick mayonnaise
1 tablespoon finely chopped onion
1 tablespoon mustard (optional)
2 tablespoons chopped chives
sea salt and milled black pepper

If the potatoes are very tiny, leave them whole. If not, slice in half. Steam, with the thyme, until tender. Turn into a bowl and toss the hot potatoes with the vinegar and some seasoning. Mix with the rest of the ingredients and check seasoning. Serve at room temperature.
For 6

potato bake

The better the potatoes, the better the bake. They're most delicious baked in cream, but you can use a rich creamy milk or even homemade chicken broth. Sometimes I simply moisten the layers of thinly sliced seasoned potatoes with olive oil, tucking in sprigs of thyme and a little crushed garlic.

1–1,5 kg large baking potatoes
50–60g butter
sea salt and milled black pepper
100–125g grated mild Gruyère (optional)
1 cup cream
1 clove garlic, crushed

Peel the potatoes and slice very thinly. Place in a bowl of water. Rub a 30cm shallow, round or oblong baking pan or dish with a little butter. Drain and dry the potatoes. Turn half of them into the prepared pan. Season, sprinkle with half the cheese (if using) and dot with half the remaining butter. Repeat. In a small saucepan, bring the cream and garlic to the boil, then pour the hot cream over the potatoes. Cover with a sheet of baking paper or aluminium foil. Bake at 190°C for 40 minutes. Remove the paper and bake for another 40 minutes or until the potatoes are very soft and the top nicely browned.
For 6–8

roast pumpkin with sage

about 2kg pumpkin
sea salt and milled black pepper
olive oil
fresh sage leaves
whole unpeeled garlic cloves

Wash the pumpkin, but don't peel it. Slice into slim wedges. Discard the seeds. Arrange in a single layer on a baking tray. Season and moisten with oil. Add a handful of sage and garlic. Roast at 200°C, one shelf above the middle, for 30 minutes or until very tender. To serve, squeeze some of the roasted garlic cloves out of the skins, mash and smear over the pumpkin.
For 6

roast chicken with honey and mustard

1 large free-range chicken, 1,5–2kg
sea salt and milled black pepper
1 bunch fresh sage leaves
1 onion, sliced into slim wedges
50g butter, melted
1 tablespoon honey
2 tablespoons coarse seed mustard

Wash, dry and season the chicken. Stuff the chicken with the bunch of sage leaves and the onion, then tie up neatly. Place on its side on a rack in a roasting tin. Roast at 220°C for 20 minutes. Turn and roast for another 20 minutes. Now place breast-side up. Mix together the butter, honey and mustard and brush over the chicken. Turn down the heat to 190°C and roast for another 20 to 30 minutes or until nicely browned and tender.

For 4

wholewheat honey rolls

2 cups warm water
2 teaspoons dried yeast
1/4 cup runny honey
2 1/4 cups cake flour
2 teaspoons salt
1 free-range egg yolk
3 cups wholewheat flour
100g butter, cut into bits
1 free-range egg, beaten with 1 tablespoon water

Pour the warm water into a large bowl. Stir in the yeast and honey. Leave to stand for 15 minutes or until frothy. Sift over 2 cups of the cake flour and the salt. Beat with a wooden spoon until smooth. Cover and leave at room temperature for 30 minutes or until risen and foamy. Beat in the egg yolk. Place the wholewheat flour in a bowl and rub in the butter. Mix into the yeast mixture, adding the rest of the cake flour (and more if necessary) to make a very soft dough. Knead well together on a very well-floured surface, lightly flouring the dough as you work. Place in an oiled bowl, turning it around to coat with the oil. Cover and leave to rise until doubled. Punch down and knead lightly. Allow to rest for 5–10 minutes before shaping. Divide the dough into 8 equal pieces and knead lightly. Shape into smooth buns and place on an oiled baking sheet. Flatten the tops with the palm of your hand. Brush with the beaten egg and water. Allow to rise for about 10 minutes. Bake at 190°C for 30 minutes or until golden brown.
Makes 8

honey-nut spread

100g pecans or walnuts
3/4 cup honey, at room temperature

Roast the nuts at 180°C for 10 minutes or until golden. Grind half the nuts finely and mix with the honey. Leave a few of the nuts whole for garnishing and chop the rest by hand to mix with the honey. Turn the honey mixture into a jar and press in the whole roasted nuts.
Makes about 1 1/2 cups

vanilla ice cream

Wash and dry scraped vanilla pods, then bury them in a jar of caster sugar to make your own vanilla sugar. It's also a good way to store whole vanilla pods before using them.

3 cups full-cream milk
1 cup cream
1 cup vanilla sugar
2–3 vanilla pods, split lengthwise
6 free-range egg yolks

STEP 1. Place the milk, cream and half the sugar in a saucepan. Scrape out the seeds from the pods and add, along with the pods. Bring to a boil and immediately remove from the heat. Cover and leave to infuse for 15 minutes.

STEP 2. Beat the egg yolks with the remaining 1/2 cup sugar until thick and pale.

STEP 3. Over a high heat bring the infused-milk mixture to a boil, stirring all the time. Remove and gradually beat into the egg-yolk mixture. Return to the saucepan and cook over a gentle heat, while stirring, for 5 minutes or until the mixture is thick enough to coat the back of a spoon. Take care not to let it boil.

STEP 4. Strain into a bowl and cool over ice, stirring now and again, until chilled. Cover and refrigerate for a day to develop the flavour. Use an ice-cream maker and freeze according to manufacturer's instructions. Alternatively, pour into a metal or strong plastic container (not more than half-full) and freeze for at least an hour or until frozen around the edge. Whisk, or use an electric hand-held blender. Return to the freezer and repeat 2 or 3 times. This should prevent ice crystals from forming and spoiling the texture.
For 8

Variation: for a richer ice cream, use 2 cups cream and 2 cups full-cream milk.

vanilla ice-cream cake with frosted blueberries

Pack vanilla ice-cream (see page 150) into a round cake tin lined with a circle of nonstick baking paper. Freeze until serving. To frost the berries, dip into lightly beaten organic egg white, then into caster sugar. Spread out to dry on a sheet of nonstick baking paper. Before serving, turn out the ice-cream layer onto a cake plate and top with the frosted berries. Cut into wedges and serve with wafer biscuits.
For 8

fresh date cheesecake

The first time I bought fresh dates in South Africa was in Velddrif. A handmade sign outside a house drew my attention to the large date palm in the garden, and I bought a branch of sweet, soft dates. Today they're plentiful at most supermarkets. The organic ones are best – plump and delicious.

For the crust, mix together:
1/2 cup biscuit crumbs
1/2 cup ground almonds
1/2 cup desiccated coconut
1/2 teaspoon ground ginger
1/2 teaspoon ground cinnamon
1/3 cup melted butter

Pat into a deep 20cm tart dish, well-buttered, or a 22–23cm loose-bottomed tart tin. Freeze while heating the oven to 200°C. Bake for 8 minutes to set the crust. Allow to cool.

For the filling:
about 12 fresh dates, pitted
3 extra-large free-range eggs
1/2 cup caster sugar
500g creamed cottage cheese
1 cup thick sour cream

Arrange the dates in the baked crust. Beat together the remaining ingredients until smooth, then pour over the dates. Bake at 150°C for about an hour or until a toothpick inserted in the middle comes out almost clean. Turn off the heat and leave the cheesecake in the oven until completely cooled.
For 8

CHAPTER SIX

picnics and trail snacks

What bliss to pack a picnic to enjoy leisurely on the beach under big umbrellas, or perched on the rocks at sundown. Tins of sandwiches, a flask of iced tea, a portable picnic cake. Take care to choose food that's easy to transport and easy to eat on the sand. There are stunning walks along the coast, an easy stroll on the beach, or a longer hike through the nature reserve. Spring, of course, is the highlight of the year, when flowers miraculously carpet the earth. Leave early and break for breakfast, hot coffee and a muffin, or something delicious for elevenses. Nothing major to carry, just small and delicious.

rosemary bread

This is one of my favourite bread recipes. If you use instant dried yeast, there's no need to prove, simply mix with the flour. You can also bake it in two square pans, or stretch it to fit a large shallow baking pan to make a flat bread.

2 teaspoons dried yeast
1 teaspoon sugar
about 1 1/3–1 1/2 cups warm water
3 cups white bread flour
1 teaspoon salt
4 tablespoons olive oil
sprigs of fresh rosemary
coarse sea salt
milled black pepper

STEP 1. Dissolve the yeast and sugar in 1/2 cup of warm water. Leave for about 10 minutes or until frothy.

STEP 2. Sift the flour and salt into a bowl. Stir in the dissolved yeast, the rest of the water and 3 table-spoons of the olive oil to make a soft dough.

STEP 3. Turn onto a well-floured board and knead for 10–15 minutes until smooth and elastic. Keep flouring your hands if necessary. Oil a large bowl and roll the ball of dough around in it. Seal the bowl with plastic film and leave to rise in a warm kitchen until doubled (about 1 1/2 hours). Punch down and knead lightly. Rest for about 5 minutes.

STEP 4. Line an oiled oblong baking pan (about 30cm x 23cm) with nonstick baking paper and spread dough to fit so that it is about 1cm thick. Press in rosemary and sprinkle with coarse salt and pepper. Dimple with the back of a wooden spoon or poke with your fingertips. Drizzle over the remaining tablespoon of oil. Cover and leave to rise again until almost doubled.

STEP 5. Bake at 200°C for 30 minutes or until golden.
For 8

wholewheat seed loaf

Visitors to the Cape always ask for the recipe for this local bread. It's a real meal of a loaf, roughly textured with the seeds and full of goodness.

3 cups wholewheat flour
1 cup oats
1/2 cup bran
1/4 cup sesame seeds
1/4 cup poppy seeds
1/4 cup linseeds
1/4 cup sunflower seeds
1 tablespoon dried yeast
1 tablespoon honey
2 cups warm water
2 teaspoons salt
1 tablespoon sunflower oil
a mix of seeds for sprinkling

Mix the flour, oats, bran and seeds in a bowl. Stir the yeast and honey into half a cup of the warm water and leave for about 10 minutes until frothy. Add the salt, oil and the bubbly yeast to the flour mixture. Stir in the rest of the warm water. Turn into a 25cm loaf pan, well-oiled and lined with baking paper or coated with a nonstick cooking spray. Sprinkle liberally with a mixture of seeds and press in with your fingertips. Leave in a warm place until risen to the top, or almost to the top, of the tin. Bake at 200°C for an hour. Turn onto a baking pan and return to the switched-off oven for 10–15 minutes to make sure that the centre is not too moist. Cool on a wire rack, covered with a tea towel, to soften the crust.
For 8

rare roast beef with mustard mayonnaise and watercress on rosemary bread

To roast the beef:
1 kg centre-cut beef fillet
1 tablespoon coarse seed mustard
1 tablespoon smooth Dijon mustard
coarsely cracked black peppercorns
olive oil
soy sauce
a few sprigs rosemary

Smear the beef with the mustards and pepper and moisten with oil and soy sauce. Leave for an hour or so at room temperature or overnight in the fridge. Place on an oiled baking pan, tucking the rosemary underneath. Roast at 230°C for 20 minutes, turning halfway, until well-browned outside and still rosy-rare inside. Remove, cover with foil and allow to rest for 10 minutes.

To make the mustard mayonnaise, mix together:
1 cup thick mayonnaise
2 tablespoons coarse seed mustard
2 tablespoons smooth Dijon mustard

To assemble the sandwiches:
rosemary bread (see page 158), watercress

Cut the bread into large squares, then slice across. Spread with mustard mayonnaise, then sandwich with sliced beef and watercress.
For 8

tarragon-chicken salad on white country bread

For the chicken salad:
500g–600g chicken breasts, skinned and boned
dry white wine or lemon juice for poaching
fresh tarragon
sea salt and milled black pepper
2 tablespoons tarragon vinegar
1/2 cup pecans
1/2 cup finely chopped celery
1/4 cup thick mayonnaise
1/4 cup Greek yoghurt

Cover the chicken breasts with half water and half wine, or simply add a good squeeze of lemon juice to some water for poaching. Add a few sprigs of tarragon and a little seasoning. Bring to the boil, then reduce the heat and simmer for 5 minutes or until springy to the touch. Allow to cool in the poaching liquid. Drain and shred. Toss with the vinegar first, then add a tablespoon of chopped tarragon and the rest of the ingredients.

To make the sandwiches:
8 slices white country bread
soft lettuce leaves or chicory leaves

Sandwich the bread together with the chicken salad and lettuce or chicory.
For 4

a meal of a salad: crunchy mixed salad with honey-yoghurt dressing

For the salad:
2 cos lettuces, roughly sliced
6–8 baby carrots, sliced lengthwise
1 baby cabbage, thinly sliced
4 small crisp cucumbers, sliced lengthwise
4–6 salad onions, sliced lengthwise
handful of baby tomatoes

6–8 baby corn, sliced lengthwise
1 sweet red pepper, thinly sliced
handful of radishes, thinly sliced
1 stick celery, peeled and sliced into strips
8 whole sugar snap peas, trimmed

For the dressing, blend together:
juice of 1 lemon
1 clove garlic, crushed
1 teaspoon honey
sea salt and milled black pepper

2/3 cup thin natural yoghurt
1 teaspoon mustard
2/3 cup sunflower oil

Toss the mix of crunchy salad ingredients together with the dressing.
For 4–6

couscous and chickpea salad

1 bag mixed salad leaves

Mix together:
2 cups freshly made still-warm couscous
1/2 cup shredded mint leaves
1 1/2 cups cooked chickpeas
1/3 cup fresh lemon juice
1/3 cup currants, soaked in boiling water and drained
1/3 cup olive oil
250g carrot strips or shreds
sea salt and milled black pepper

Add a good handful of mixed salad leaves to the tossed couscous-and-chickpea mix.
For 8

olive spread, roasted vegetables, parmesan and rocket on rosemary bread

For the olive spread, pound together:
2 cups pitted black olives
2 tablespoons capers, rinsed
6 anchovy fillets, chopped
2 cloves garlic, crushed
squeeze of lemon juice
1/2 cup olive oil
1 teaspoon dried oregano
twist of black pepper

For the roasted vegetables:
4 small eggplants, thinly sliced lengthways   **2 sweet red peppers**
2 sweet yellow peppers   **olive oil**

Salt the eggplant slices and place in a colander for half an hour. Rinse and pat dry. Halve, core and seed the peppers. Arrange, cut-side down, on an oiled baking tray. Add the slices of eggplant, all in a single layer. Moisten with olive oil. Roast the eggplant at 200°C for 10–15 minutes and the peppers for 30–40 minutes or until tender and starting to catch. Once cool, skin the peppers. If made ahead of time, pack the vegetables into a jar, well covered with olive oil. Store in the fridge, but bring to room temperature before serving. Any leftover oil can be used for salad dressings.

To assemble the sandwiches:
rosemary bread (see page 158), rocket, shavings of Parmesan cheese

Cut the bread into large squares, then slice across. Cover the cut sides with the olive spread, then sandwich with roasted vegetables, shavings of Parmesan and rocket.
For 8

marinated mushroom and mozzarella sandwiches

250g portabellini mushrooms, cleaned and sliced
200g soft mozzarella ball, torn into shreds
basil leaves

For the marinade, mix together:
1/2 cup olive oil
juice of 1 large lemon
1 clove garlic, crushed
sea salt and milled black pepper

Mix the mushrooms and mozzarella with the marinade. Leave for a few hours or overnight in the fridge. Use as a sandwich filling together with the basil leaves.
For 4

smoked snoek and avocado tabbouleh

1 cup bulgur or cracked wheat
250g smoked snoek, flaked
3 medium, firm red tomatoes, seeded and chopped
5–6 tablespoons olive oil
1 firm ripe avocado, skinned and chopped
4 tablespoons fresh lemon juice
250g crisp baby cucumbers, chopped
1 bunch spring onions, chopped
1 cup chopped mixed fresh herbs (mix of Italian parsley, mint, coriander and dill)
salt and milled black pepper
soft butter-lettuce leaves

Pour boiling water over the bulgur wheat and leave to stand for 30 minutes. Drain well. Mix the wheat together with the flaked snoek, chopped ingredients, oil and lemon juice, and season to taste. Spoon into lettuce cups to serve.
For 6

egg salad and lettuce on wholewheat bread

For the egg salad, mix together:
6 hard-boiled eggs, chopped
1/2 cup thick mayonnaise
6–8 spring onions, chopped
sea salt and milled black pepper

To assemble the sandwiches:
8 slices wholewheat bread (see page 161)
soft lettuce leaves

Sandwich slices of wholewheat bread with egg salad and lettuce leaves.
For 4

paprika cream cheese spread on rye bread

For the cream cheese spread:
250g low-fat cream cheese
100g butter
2 tablespoons finely chopped onion
1 teaspoon caraway seeds
1 tablespoon sweet paprika
1 teaspoon chopped capers
1 teaspoon dry mustard
1/3 cup thick sour cream or crème fraîche
salt and milled black pepper

Bring cream cheese and butter to room temperature, then cream together until smooth. Mix in the remaining ingredients, seasoning to taste. Chill to firm to a good spreadable consistency.

To assemble the sandwiches:
sliced rye (or wholewheat) bread, sliced radishes, pickled or fresh crisp cucumbers, whole spring onions

Thickly spread the bread with the cheese spread and sandwich with sliced cucumbers, sliced radishes and whole spring onions.
For 8

avocado and goats' milk cheese on wholewheat honey rolls

4 ripe avocados
juice of 2 lemons
sea salt and milled black pepper
8 thick slices soft goats' milk cheese
1/4 cup olive oil
1 tablespoon chopped chives
8 wholewheat honey rolls (see page 148)
butter, at room temperature
fresh sprouts
8 or more large soft lettuce leaves

Thinly slice the avocados and marinate in the lemon juice and some seasoning for about 20 minutes.
Marinate the goats' milk cheese in the olive oil with the chives and some seasoning. Split the rolls and
butter them. Sandwich with the avocado, cheese, sprouts and lettuce leaves.
For 8

iced orange and cinnamon tea

4 rooibos tea bags
2 sticks cinnamon
2 cups boiling water
2 cups iced water
2 cups strained fresh orange juice
ice cubes
fresh mint
honey (optional)

Steep the tea bags and cinnamon in the boiling water for a full 5 minutes to release the flavours. Discard
the tea bags and cinnamon and mix with the iced water and orange juice. Refrigerate until well chilled.
Serve over ice, adding a sprig or two of mint. If you like it sweeter, stir in some honey.
For 6

picnic cake

1/2 cup dried fruitcake mix
1/4 cup brandy
2 1/4 cups flour
1 teaspoon baking powder
1/4 teaspoon salt
2/3 cup caster sugar
200g soft unsalted butter
1 tablespoon sunflower oil
1 extra-large free-range egg, beaten
3 free-range egg yolks
icing sugar

Pour boiling water over the fruitcake mix, drain well, and steep in the brandy for an hour or so. Sift the flour, baking powder and salt into a bowl. Mix in the sugar, then beat in the butter and the oil. Beat in the beaten whole egg and the yolks. Fold in the soaked fruit and brandy. Turn into a well-buttered 20cm layer-cake tin lined with a circle of nonstick baking paper. Bake at 180°C for 40–45 minutes or until golden brown and a tester inserted comes out clean. Cool slightly before turning onto a wire rack. Once completely cooled, sift icing sugar over.
For 8

chorizo, sun-dried tomato and olive muffins

100g chorizo salami or sausage
50g sun-dried tomatoes
1/3 cup olives (packed)
2–3 tablespoons chopped Italian parsley
1 3/4 cups flour
2 teaspoons baking powder
1/4 teaspoon salt
4 free-range eggs, lightly beaten
1/2 cup good olive oil
1/4 cup dry white wine
milled black pepper

Chop the chorizo. Pour boiling water over the tomatoes and leave for 10–15 minutes. Drain and chop. Smash the olives and remove the pips. Chop roughly. Mix the chopped ingredients with the parsley. Sift the flour with the baking powder and salt. Add the eggs, oil and wine and beat well together. Mix in the chopped ingredients, adding a twist of black pepper. Coat 10–12 muffin pans with nonstick cooking spray. Spoon in the batter and bake at 200°C for about 20 minutes or until golden and baked through. Rest for a few minutes, then turn out and serve while still warm.
Makes 10–12

blueberry buttermilk muffins

2 cups cake flour
4 teaspoons baking powder
1/2 teaspoon salt
2 tablespoons caster sugar
125g very cold butter
1 extra-large free-range egg
1 cup buttermilk
125g blueberries, fresh or frozen

Sift the flour with the baking powder and salt. Stir in the sugar. Grate in the butter and rub lightly with the fingertips until crumbly. Beat the egg with the buttermilk and stir into the flour mixture until just moistened but still lumpy. Mix in half the blueberries (don't defrost the frozen ones). Spoon the mixture into 12 muffin pans coated with nonstick cooking spray or lined with squares of nonstick baking paper. Press in the rest of the berries. Bake at 220°C for 15 minutes or until risen and browned.
Makes 12

carrot and bran muffins

1/4 cup sunflower oil
1/3 cup brown sugar
2 extra-large free-range eggs
1 cup grated carrots
1 1/4 cups wholewheat flour
1 teaspoon bicarbonate of soda
1 teaspoon baking powder
1/2 teaspoon salt
1 teaspoon cinnamon
1/2 teaspoon ground nutmeg
1 1/4 cups bran cereal flakes
1/4 cup seedless raisins
1/4 cup chopped pecans
3/4 cup buttermilk

Mix the oil and sugar together in a large bowl. Beat in the eggs until foamy, then stir in the grated carrots. Sift together the flour, bicarbonate of soda, baking powder, salt and spices. Tip in the bran that's left behind in the sieve. Add to the carrot mixture, then add the bran flakes, raisins, pecans and buttermilk, stirring until just combined. Be careful not to overmix. Spoon into 10–12 muffin pans coated with a nonstick cooking spray. Bake at 200°C for 20 minutes or until risen and done. These are at their best freshly baked, split and spread with smooth cream cheese.
Makes 10–12

date, oat and coconut bars

250g chopped pitted dates
1 cup oats
1 cup desiccated coconut
2 tablespoons sunflower oil
2 tablespoons honey
1/4 cup melted butter
1/2 cup fresh orange juice
1/2 cup wholewheat flour
1 teaspoon bicarbonate of soda
1 teaspoon mixed spice

Mix together the dates, oats and coconut. Mix together the oil, honey, butter and orange juice, then stir into the date mixture. Mix together the flour, bicarbonate of soda and mixed spice and mix well with the date mixture. Press into a 20cm-square baking pan coated with nonstick cooking spray or lined with nonstick baking paper. Spread out evenly. Bake at 180°C for 25–30 minutes or until golden brown and set. Allow to cool in the tin before cutting into bars.
Makes 18

bush tea fruit bread

250g fruitcake mixture
2 1/2 cups hot rooibos or honeybush tea
1 tablespoon honey
1 cup sifted cake flour
2 cups wholewheat flour
1 tablespoon instant dried yeast
1 cup bran
2 teaspoons salt
1/4 cup chopped pecans (optional)

Pour boiling water over the fruitcake mixture and drain. Place in a bowl and pour over the hot tea. Stir in the honey. Leave to steep for about 15 minutes or until hand-hot. Mix the flours, yeast, bran and salt in a bowl. Mix in the fruit and tea, and the pecans if using. If the mixture seems too stiff, stir in a little warm water. Spoon into a loaf tin, oiled or coated with nonstick cooking spray and lined with a strip of baking paper. Leave in a warm spot in the kitchen for about 15 minutes until risen to the top. Bake at 200°C for an hour. Cool for 10–15 minutes, covered with a tea towel. Invert onto a baking tray and return to the switched-off but still-warm oven for 10–15 minutes.
For 8

conversion table

• The tablespoons used throughout the book are 15ml, the teaspoons are 5ml.
They are always level measurements.
• All eggs are extra-large unless otherwise stated.
• When a dish is cooked in the oven, always use the middle shelf unless otherwise stated.

measurements

STANDARD	METRIC
1/4 inch	5mm
1/2 inch	1cm
1 inch	2,5cm
2 inches	5cm
3 inches	7cm
4 inches	10cm
5 inches	12cm
6 inches	15cm
7 inches	18cm
8 inches	20cm
9 inches	23cm
10 inches	25cm
11 inches	28cm
12 inches	30cm

liquid measure

STANDARD	METRIC
1 teaspoon	5ml
1 tablespoon	15ml
1/4 cup	60ml
1/3 cup	80ml
1/2 cup	125ml
2/3 cup	160ml
3/4 cup	175ml
3/4 cup	180ml
1 cup	250ml
1 1/4 cups	300ml
1 1/2 cups	375ml
1 2/3 cups	400ml
1 3/4 cups	450ml
2 cups	500ml
2 1/2 cups	600ml
3 cups	750ml

weight

STANDARD	METRIC
1/2 oz	15g
1 oz	30g
2 oz	60g
3 oz	90g
4 oz	125g
6 oz	175g
8 oz	250g
10 oz	300g
12 oz	375g
13 oz	400g
14 oz	425g
1 lb	500g
1 1/2 lb	750g
2 lb	1 kg

oven temperatures

FAHRENHEIT	CELSIUS	DESCRIPTION
225°F	110°C	COOL
250°F	120°C	COOL
275°F	140°C	VERY SLOW
300°F	150°C	VERY SLOW
325°F	160°C	SLOW
350°F	180°C	MODERATE
375°F	190°C	MODERATE
400°F	200°C	MODERATELY HOT
425°F	220°C	HOT
450°F	230°C	HOT

**QUIVERTREE
PUBLICATIONS**

RECIPES PHILLIPPA CHEIFITZ **PHOTOGRAPHS** CRAIG FRASER
EDITORS ROBYN ALEXANDER & NANCY RICHARDS **DESIGN & PRODUCTION** LIBBY DOYLE
PROPS ANDRÉ CROUSE OF PLUSH BAZAAR **SCANNING** RAY'S PHOTO CONTROL

PUBLISHED BY QUIVERTREE PUBLICATIONS, SOUTH AFRICA
PO BOX 51051 • WATERFRONT • 8002 • CAPE TOWN • SOUTH AFRICA
TEL: +27 (0) 21 461 6808 • FAX: +27 (0) 21 461 6842 • E-MAIL: info@quivertree.co.za

www.quivertree.co.za

ISBN-13: 978-0-620-35836-1
ISBN-10: 0-620-35836-X